reclaiming our stories
IN THE TIME OF COVID AND UPRISING

reclaiming our stories
IN THE TIME OF COVID AND UPRISING

editors:
Paul Khalid Alexander
Manuel Paul López
Darius Spearman
Ebony Tyree

**SD
CWP**

**SAN DIEGO
CITY WORKS
PRESS**

ISBN 978-0-9837837-4-9
Library of Congress Control Number: 2021944401

San Diego City Works Press is a non-profit press, funded by local writers and friends of the arts, committed to the publication of fiction, poetry, creative nonfiction, and art by members of the San Diego City College community and the community at large. For more about San Diego City Works Press, please visit our website at www.cityworkspress.org.

San Diego City Works Press is extremely indebted to the American Federation of Teachers, Local 1931, without whose generous contribution and commitment to the arts this book would not be possible.

Cover design: Rondi Vasquez
Cover photo: Jason Stanton-Milsap
Production editor: Will Dalrymple | Layout & Editing | willdalrymple.com

Published in the United States by San Diego City Works Press, California
Printed in the United States of America

dedication

We celebrate this special edition while mourning the loss of Samantha Jasmine Thornton, one of our Reclaiming Our Stories family, to cancer last year. Samantha, also known lovingly as "Sam," was one of our first community members to share her story with a cohort but quickly became one of our teachers in life. In her story published in our first book, she introduced us all to her son "Sweet Pea." He died at a young age, also from cancer, with his mother loving on him and brightening his life the way she did ours. Every chance she got she made it clear that his short life was a cause for celebration. It was not a reason to mourn. The joy with which she spoke of him made us all realize how precious life is. And the tears that fell down people's cheeks as she read her story continue to be a testimony to the pain she must have felt at his loss when no one was around. We are still in awe at her strength, her resilience, and her joy.

In the last few months of her life, while undergoing chemotherapy, she would show up at events despite our pleas for her to stay home and rest. We asked her to stay home but were always glad when she came anyway. Being in her presence felt good. She understood the value of friendship, of struggle, and she understood the value of life. As one of our first authors for Reclaiming Our Stories, she gave strength and comfort to everyone in her cohort. She was full of love and kindness and helped all of our authors recognize that their stories mattered, that they too, through their stories, had much to offer the world.

The sign of a real teacher is their ability to impart lessons through their actions to those who know them. So, perhaps the best way to honor

Samantha is to incorporate the joy and love that she had for her son into our own lives and memories of her. Samantha, we want you to know that we were listening and that we saw you. We saw your life, and we saw your love, and we want you to know that we were paying attention. We were taking notes. To Samantha, aka Mz Blessed Like That, aka The Champ, thank you for sharing your story with us, and thank you for all of your lessons. Thank you for being you and for allowing us to be inspired and learn from the life you lived.

table of contents

the stories

foreword
The Multiple Pandemics and Why We Fight
Roberto D. Hernández

As this special edition of *Reclaiming Our Stories* reclaims our narratives of struggle and resiliency, dissension and dignity, it also provides us the opportunity to reflect on the ongoing pandemic, the recent 2020 presidential elections, and the debacle that has ensued. In other words, this book gives us the opportunity to reflect on the stories this nation tells itself about itself and the tales we use to deceive ourselves into believing that the United States is a beacon of freedom for the world and place of progress and opportunity, as opposed to a nightmare that continues to be marked by the racist and sexist foundations upon which it is built. This volume, created by San Diego's Pillars of the Community, adds to the recounting of stories from the front lines of the pandemic and the fight for racial justice. But first, some contextualization seems in order.

November 4th, 2008, as voting booths began to close, it became increasingly clear that voters had placed the first-ever non-white male in the White House. Barack Hussein Obama was elected to be the first Black president of the United States. On that day, millions shed tears for the historic victory, me included. However, we did not get to inauguration day without a tragic reminder that the history of racism in the United States was alive and well. The new year, the "new era," would begin with bloodshed.

In the early hours of January 1, 2009, a 22-year-old father of one, Oscar Grant III, was shot and killed by Bay Area Rapid Transit (BART) Police on the platform of Fruitvale Station in Oakland, California. He was killed execution style while he lay face down and restrained. The officer would later claim he only wanted to taze the restrained young man. As if that were any better. Ironically, Grant—who having opted to be responsible and use public transit to commute to and from New Year's Eve festivities that previous night with his friends, a group of Black and Brown young men—would end up becoming the first of many high-profile killings of unarmed young Black and Brown men and women at the hands of police, whose executions went viral after being caught on camera. In fact, between the murder of Oscar Grant and the public execution of George Floyd, multiple names have been added to this list: Tamir Rice, Andrés Guardado, Michael Brown, Philando Castille, Sergio Weick, Breonna Taylor, Sandra Bland, Tony McDade, Jonathon Coronel, Sean Monterrosa, and countless others. Attention to the killing of Black and Brown peoples, while endemic to the history of racial/ colonial and gendered violence in the US, has been unprecedented. But importantly, Black and Brown resistance and solidarity has also grown exponentially.

While Black Lives Matter, as both hashtag and movement, took shape following the deaths of Michael Brown and Trayvon Martin to bring attention to police impunity, it is important to remember what some have called the Oakland Rebellions of 2009. The solidarity on the platform of BART on that fateful day, and the "riots" that followed in the weeks to come, ultimately led to the BART officer becoming the first-ever law enforcement officer in the history of California to be arrested and charged with murder for a killing that occurred while on duty. Legal action and repercussions against officers involved in shootings have been strongest when the response on the streets has been the most widespread and determined. While far too many officers have gone without charges, the killing of George Floyd—which sparked worldwide protests amidst a pandemic!—continues to exemplify that when Black and Brown communities come together in principled unity against injustice, as opposed to just a Black or Brown face in a high place, direct action gets the goods. This too was the case in La Mesa when, in the midst of the George Floyd outrage, San Diego County witnessed a La Mesa police officer physically assault Amaurie Johnson and took to the streets in protest.

My closest comrades and I—or *compas* as we say in Spanish—were in the streets in both instances: in Oakland following the killing of Oscar Grant and in La Mesa and San Diego following the killing of George Floyd, as we had been in El Cajon following the police murder of Alfred Olango some years back. We have seen both the police injustice of killing unarmed Black and Brown folks, the continued caging of Black and Brown asylum seekers, and the repressive response when communities come together to challenge such abuses of power and utter disregard for our lives. We witnessed dignified and righteous anger take the Interstate 8. The largest, most unexpected and effective actions in recent San Diego history got the LMPD officer responsible for harassing Amaurie Johnson fired, but only after the Chase and Union Banks were up in flames. Amidst the protests nationwide some argued marches and actions must follow community leadership, yet in some instances this leadership led to a staged hug-a-cop-a-thon or photo-op with a kneeling officer. Flash, flash, cameras are gone, and the killing continues. Community representation without principled politics, and true justice as its guide, does not matter if state-sanctioned violence continues.

The stories in this volume relate to the real-life experiences of those on the front lines and often on the receiving end of state-sanctioned and/or extralegal violence that has shaped the history of this nation. Yet, in the thick of the flames, Christina M. Kelley reveals how as a nurse she found her purpose fighting for justice as a street medic, tending to those who refuse to go along to get along. Anne Marie Rios, Leslie Furcron and Ismahan Abdullahi recount the role of Faith in seeking justice, in providing one with strength and spiritual fortitude when facing the diverse forms of state violence that are dished out against communities of color. Whether in the streets or in detention centers, in fleeing persecution abroad or fleeing those who are supposed to "protect and serve," their testimonies provide us a roadmap during these challenging times. Briseida Salazar and Zack Dowdy detail stories of unity in action—solidarity across linguistic and racial borders alike—in a private, for-profit immigrant detention facility and rolling down 6th Avenue in a sea of skaters. These stories serve as backdrop for this ongoing pandemic. They are stories that provide the substance of who we collectively are.

As of this writing, number 45 stands to be a one-term president. Yet, his own delusion and self-deception have not ended. He continues to refuse to concede. While pundits debate the new normal and forecast the future, kids are still in cages, and unarmed Black and Brown people continue to be killed by police.

Yes, in this century we have seen more Black and Brown faces in elected positions of power; however, representation without principled politics, and true justice as its guide, does not matter if state-sanctioned violence against our communities persists. We must continue to reclaim our stories and our power.

the background
Pillars of the Community and the Reclaiming Our Stories Project

Pillars of the Community began with a few Muslims and an intention to build a support system for people returning home to Southeast San Diego after incarceration. Southeast had and continues to have one of the highest incarceration rates in the county and has long suffered from neglect at the hands of politicians and large non-profit organizations. We recognized that in order to build this community, the people closest to the pain—who were typically overlooked and dismissed—must become (and often already were) the "Pillars" of the community.

Currently, most of our work is done through community building (pushing positivity), assisting individuals negatively impacted by the criminal justice system, and policy advocacy work. Whether through legislation around gang documentation, speaking up at town hall meetings, or in exposing racial profiling, Pillars has slowly become an influential voice in San Diego politics.

The Reclaiming Our Stories project was first launched in the summer of 2015. The original idea behind Reclaiming Our Stories (ROS) was to create an environment where community members could come together to share their stories with friends and family and celebrate how amazing they were. Although many of the stories were about traumatic events in their lives, the fact that they had overcome those events was a testament to their strength and resilience. In the months that we worked together, we built a trusting community of writers, and by finally reading their stories to an audience, most of our writers recognized and expressed that the experience had in many ways been both cathartic and healing. Finally, City Works Press expressed interest in this collection of stories and eventually published the first two volumes.

preface
Reclaiming Our Stories: Pandemic and Uprising

This special edition of *Reclaiming Our Stories*, unlike our previous two volumes, is a *theme-based* collection focusing on the first year of the COVID-19 pandemic as well as the massive uprising across the United States against police brutality.

Each voice in this volume is an invaluable contribution to the collective chorus of resistance. A chorus that requires many voices, and one that must be sustained and full-throated if we are ever to see a significant change in this country. Our goal has been to capture these lived experiences while still fresh in the minds and hearts of these authors.

We originally came together on six Zoom meetings, first as a group to tell our stories, and then to present them to our friends and family members, again on Zoom. We were not able to meet in person, but we bonded together as we listened to each other's experiences. Our storytellers frequently recounted organizing and participating in protests, suffering unwarranted police violence, managing family trauma, deaths and disease of loved ones, serving as health workers in the middle of the pandemic, and sometimes simply sharing their personal reflections of day-to-day coping and pain.

With this project, our goal was not only to document the turbulence and heat of this unprecedented moment but also to capture the bravery exhibited by so many among us. Reader, it is not just our hope that you can find your way into these stories but that you can contribute one of your own when the time is right for you.

acknowledgments

We'd like to offer our unyielding gratitude to Roberta Alexander. Your guidance and excitement about this project have been a major force since its beginning. Thank you to Will Dalrymple and Rondi Vasquez. It's with a collaborative spirit and keen sensibilities that you have produced books that are not only engaging texts to read but beautiful artifacts to hold in the hands. We'd also like to shout out Kelly Mayhew and Jim Miller, City Works Press managing editors, for your ongoing support. Thank you to Greg Sarris, Linda Sarsour, Dr. Rudolf Ware, and Daniel Widener for your empowering words and the tireless work you do. We can't thank you enough. Special thanks to Roberto D. Hernández and Darius Spearman. The context you have provided addresses what's at stake and how we have arrived at this moment. Finally, we offer an immense thank you to all of the readers and supporters of City Works Press. Without you, this volume would not be possible.

the stories

Christina M. Kelley is a Critical Care Advanced Practice Nurse operationalizing the nursing code of ethics to combat public health disparities caused by systemic racism.

Christina M. Kelley
Here's to 2020

The World Health Organization designated 2020 the International Year of the Nurse to commemorate the 200th anniversary of Florence Nightingale's birth, but it quickly became the year of the global pandemic, open racism, and social uprising. COVID-19 became real on a rainy night in early March while I sat in an Indianapolis hotel room. The United States was put on notice that COVID-19 was here, and we were going to need to deal with its presence. What was supposed to be a massive networking opportunity for nurse leaders turned into a large group of professionals who were wide-eyed and terrified, second guessing their choice to travel and concerned about returning home safely. Every one of us was thinking, I should have been smarter than this, I should have known better, I am a nurse. I thought to myself, Am I taking illness home to my loved ones? I was among that number of conference-goers scolding myself for having left my family to travel for professional development. Coronavirus was in Europe and Asia. We were supposed to be safe here, right? As I reflected on my stupidity, my phone began to ring, text messages flew in, and email notifications sent my phone buzzing. It was work; it was recall time. Get home ASAP, the messages read. My direct flight was cancelled. It took four flights, three layovers, crowded airports, lines, packed terminals, tons of hand sanitizer, an entire roll of Lysol wipes, and 16 hours later my husband and kiddo arrived to pick me up from the airport, and I didn't even want to get in the car. Was I infected?

I got back to work the next day, and our ICU was under construction. Regular rooms were turned into negative pressure rooms to combat the spread of the virus. Information from our most trusted organizations changed by the hour. Team members were shell-shocked, but the worst was yet to come. Where the hell was our PPE? "No mask, no worries, just wear a bandana, what could go wrong?" the CDC said. The government had abandoned us, and the Center for Disease Control and Prevention had failed us. Families were barred from entering the hospital. No visitors were allowed. All points of entry were locked down, and security was manning the main entrance. That was a nurse's dream, because we could now work in peace. We were happy in our thoughts of a family-and-question-free work environment, but that dream quickly turned into a nightmare when the dying started, so much death. Our ICU was turned into a reluctant hospice house. Families screamed in disbelief, pain, and grief, trying to kiss their loved ones through the phone as they passed on from this world with only their nurse covered in head-to-toe personal protective gear to bear witness. Loved ones on IPADs outside the hospital begged their kids, husbands, wives, siblings, and friends to stay. "Just hold on," they yelled, "I'm not ready to be without you."

Even in the midst of that chaotic environment, we began planning for the surge—that theoretical occurrence that would bring in more and more infected patients. We needed to prepare for the day when nurses would have to take care of more patients than they could safely handle. We were planning to break state-mandated nurse-to-patient ratios. Can we keep ourselves and our patients safe? Our action planning became far more morbid and sobering as leadership teams began to have surreal conversations about which patients would get the ventilators and other life-sustaining resources. I thought, how do we choose?

Utilitarianism took center stage with the goal being to triage COVID-19 positive patients to allow the young, healthy, and fit to prevail. The virus, which disproportionally affects the people that suffer the most from health-related disparities, was ravaging the community. These people were my people, my Black and Brown people. They were me. Knowing that they would not be receiving the resources needed to survive made me viscerally sick every day. (How many straight days of work has it been since? I've lost count.)

As if 2020 couldn't get any worse, George Floyd was killed on live stream. My heart and head exploded. Is this what compounded trauma feels like? The world was dying, the country was raging, San Diego was rumbling, and I was on fire. I needed to bear witness to what was occurring on the street. I had never participated in a protest before and the unknown caused feelings of apprehension and fear, but I was determined. The impulse to join a movement had never crossed my mind before, not because I wasn't enraged by previous acts of police brutality or racism but because I didn't know what my individualized effort or presence could contribute. I didn't know if the call to action as a nurse during the pandemic increased my courage, but I felt bold and ready for whatever may come. During this first encounter with protest culture, I was empowered and horrified by what I saw and experienced. A quiet protest continued to grow and swell with people who were angry, tired, and resentful of the way that people of color were mistreated and manhandled. The pulsing crowd wielded signs, raised fists toward the sky in solidarity, and chanted, "THIS IS WHAT DEMOCRACY LOOKS LIKE!"

It was a warm day and the sun was throwing heat off the black asphalt of the downtown streets. People were wiping sweat off their brows and upper lips, folks were sharing water, and there was no hand sanitizer in sight. Then, watching two obvious friends embrace each other made my nursing sense tingle. I felt like I had been slapped in the face. I was so wrapped up in the movement that, for a brief moment, I had lost sight of the pandemic. Was I a hypocrite for being out in the street, shoulder to shoulder with people I didn't know, some masked, some not, some close, some distancing? Just stop! I shouted to myself. This was where I needed to be, in that moment, at that juncture, in front of the rising tower of the

Hall of Justice. I redirected my thoughts from COVID-19 to the other beast that was placing Black and Brown lives at risk—the ever-present, never-wavering, phenomenon of racism. How fitting was it to be in front of the Hall of Justice demanding justice, but there was no justice to be had that day.

The police arrived. Wait, the military? No, it was the police, just in militarized costumes, prepared for war. Who did they think was at this demonstration? Armed combatants? There were families, children, young people, professionals... nurses. The common denominator among all of these people was that they were Black and Brown. Fifty, 100, almost 150 paramilitary-gear-laden police officers arrived in waves of vehicles. These cowards cordoned off the east and west egress routes on W. Broadway to kettle us in, a tactic used to confine a group of demonstrators or protesters to a small area, as a method of crowd control. Even if a demonstrator wanted to leave there was no way out, to the North and South were buildings with no exit routes. As they marched toward the crowd, their batons were out, held tightly in leather-gloved hands. They moved forward like a wall of black steel, marching in lockstep toward the crowd. This scene would be impressive if it weren't so disturbing, knowing that they were marching toward the people that they were duty-bound to protect. This militarized force was not there to reason or collaborate. Their goal was to intimidate. It quickly became clear there would be no regard for life or limb, purpose or justice, just property protection and authoritarian rule.

The first flash-bang eruption tore through the already noisy city block. Demonstrators clapped their hands to the sides of their heads to shield their ears. I did the same. I felt like my ears had exploded, and my instinct was to take cover, then run! Looking around, I realized that others felt the same way. Many were ringing their ears with their index fingers while crouched low to the ground, while others ran to find safety. A split-second later the wispy white fog of tear-gas was visible in the air. Screaming, coughing, running, and falling ensued. My head darted around as I tried to take in visually as much as I could to assess the situation. Was this real life? My nurse sense tingled a second time that day. All I could think about was the potential for injury. There was no way in and no way out, so how could emergency medical services get to injured protestors? They couldn't, and perhaps that was the goal? As the standoff continued, the feelings of betrayal ripped through me. All I could think was that they injured you and then kept help from reaching you? Fuck that! It was time to mobilize!

This is not what I envisioned the Year of the Nurse to look like. I expected a year of celebration not a pandemic, police brutality, and a country divided. It was time to rewrite my vision of how I operationalize my nursing skills in 2020. The goal was to weaponize my nursing privilege to take aid and education to the streets, to my people. Twenty-four hours after attending my first protest, three colleagues and I committed to building a team that would support the movement and provide medical treatment on the ground. Thirty-six hours after attending my first protest, our group, which consisted of a handful of nurses, grew to a consortium of 75 medical professionals. Forty-eight hours after attending my first protest, a cross-section of our team held the line behind the protestors, creating space between them and the wolves dressed in police clothing. Ninety-six hours after attending my first protest thousands of people converged on downtown San Diego. The march was a long 10 miles, my medical pack was heavy, the noise emanating from this mass of people was deafening, but the message was clear, that justice would prevail! While watching the sea of people, I realized how much work needed to be done, but I was filled with hope.

Sunglasses and a mask hid my tears.

Anne is Helen's daughter and Daniel's mom. She is from Southeast San Diego. She is an attorney and an activist.

Anne Marie Rios

My Heart Has a River in It

When I am nervous, my hand reaches for the chain around my neck. A small pendant rests in my fingers and decades of my life float in my palm. I stare out the front window and grasp La Virgen, a gift when I turned 15. A reminder of my mother. There are days when I am afraid I will forget the way her hands felt, but this pendant was placed around me more than 25 years ago in a moment, before my party, when only she and I were together. And I am reminded not only of something as simple as her hands but of her infinite protection. For a moment my breath stops and I wonder, sitting here, now, how will I ever tell her that her hair was soft silk, that her skin was the color of precious wet sand, that my eyes memorized her face so my child's children will know her. Just as quickly, the thought fades. But not the grief. The grief stays.

I open the car door and head towards the building. There are small plants in front that can fool you into thinking this is a place with color. My heels click against the black asphalt of the parking lot, onto the concrete sidewalk. I must stop at the electric fence. At the metal. At the barbed wires. Through a noisy intercom a woman yells at me to identify myself and tell her if I have any contraband. "Cell phone, tobacco products?" she asks me in a voice I have come to recognize. I have one answer: "Legal." That at least gets me through the gateway.

I enter inside and the news is on a television with images of men that make my blood fire. It is always the same channel, always the same pro-president propaganda. I look away so as not to get angrier. I walk in and hear the guard telling the family at the front desk that he does not speak Spanish. That he cannot help. That he does not know where their brother is. I stop, place my identification cards on the counter and ask the woman who she is looking for. I speak to her in Spanish. "Con qué le puedo ayudar?" The language serving as my shield and knife against this guard that is annoyed. He rolls his eyes at the fact that I took the time to care. "No se donde está mi hermano. Lo ando buscando. No sé. No sé." "Dame el nombre de su hermano, lo vamos a encontrar." I translate for the guard and wait. For anything. Waiting is what we do here.

After the guard stares at my bar card long enough to acknowledge I really am an attorney, I have to take off my shoes. I take them off and they go through the X-ray. I go through the scanner as well. As I walk through, I feel my muscles and blood. I feel my ligaments. I feel my body dropping pieces of me as I enter.

I wait again. I must be escorted upstairs where I will wait in a lobby. They must check me in. That large square room holds people that are waiting for court. The air stands still in that room. We are all scared in that room. It is the holding space where dreams have not vanished just yet. Before we see the judge who will tell us yes or no, stay or go. I never tell anyone how scared I am in that room. How my stomach comes up my throat. I stand perfectly poised in my suit, my face with a slight smile but my heart races always. My leg shakes in a new anxious twitch I have grown slightly accustomed to.

A small gift today is that I do not have court. Instead, it is a meeting with a client. I am escorted by a guard through a small door that requires permission to enter. And then I wait...again, in a lobby with others who have lost their bodies too. In the spaces that I have waited and moved and shed pieces of myself, I have seen nothing but brown bodies. Brown bodies that escort me, brown bodies that have handcuffs, that have hard shoes on, brown bodies in uniform. Uniforms. Because there are also brown bodies that clean. Brown bodies that shuffle to and from places. Brown bodies that are prisoners on stolen land. It is not enough that they are captured and brought here, but they must serve as the cleaning staff, the cooks, the prey. They must serve themselves on a platter every dinner.

I wait and wait. Hours go by in the larger room with others, and finally a guard will yell at my client to come out of the holding room and into a private one. Then they will scream out their name again to let me know I can go too. I enter the small, sterile room. There is a table and one, two chairs. Just enough space for us to fit in. The walls are white. That white is so loud and so bland and so suffocating neither of us can exist here with it. Where there is just blankness, and the oppression. Loud and silencing. One that offends our spaces and calm. It reminds me, here, that we don't belong. That we don't belong here. Or maybe it is the white that doesn't belong.

I think of all of this as I work from home staring at my computer. I think of the last client I helped in person before the disease, which strips us of our right to breathe, has taken over hundreds of thousands of people. Each one who has died—a mother, father, sister, brother, person. A life. Like my mother's. Now, during this pandemic, I primarily talk to my clients through the phone. I must hear their stories over lines that are disrupted. Told they must put more money on their books, even though this is a legal call. Even though freedom should be free. I hear the panic in their voices rise when it is one case, two cases, fifty cases, one hundred, two hundred. For the longest time, Otay Mesa had the largest COVID-19 population of infected migrants. I hear the panic when they tell me they are scared. That their friends are quarantined. That they will be next. A private prison doesn't make money when they release people. They do make money, however, keeping them until they die. And then someone does die. He dies alone in a hospital bed. And his sister cries. I am reminded of what it felt like when I saw my mom, without breath. For just a moment, I lose my own ability to breathe. People tell us all day long, again and again and again: "No me quiero morir."

Just like she did. My last client, the client who existed before these times. She had been abused by a man who strangled her, who beat her, who tried to rip a baby from her womb. She was beat by his mother. She was told she belonged to him, that he owned her.

And she looks at me, and I tell her, you can trust me. You can. And when I ask you why you didn't leave you tell me where would you go? Who would believe you? And when I ask you why you can't return to Mexico you tell me nothing would be different. He would find you, he would kill you. The police never helped you. The three times you went, with bruises on your face, they sent you away. They laughed at you. When ICE picked you up, your body had bruises on its legs from when he pried them open, on your arms where he hit you and held you down. With your arms you took off your clothes in the van they were set to deport you in, and told them: "Look at me, look at me. If you send me with him, he will kill me."

And I am reminded of arms that have scars from where the first asylum seeker I met tried to cut her own skin off for loving women. Her tears are traces of the journey she took through Central America to escape the threats of rape. Rape that would make her a "real woman." Her pauses are canyons where most of her heart has fallen into. She describes the names police would call her when they threatened her with death. You have never had a relationship with a woman because you never wanted to believe that you could. I listen to her words in this courtroom that holds sadness and grief and pain and longing. In this box where people cry about their lives and are judged on a ten percent chance that their hurt is enough to allow them to stay. I don't know when I stop. But when I start to breathe again, I can't stop thinking about your body with so many scars on it.

And I'm reminded of a mother's description of the border where there are too many people and not enough hands. Not enough arms to hold onto your three children. That she is scared. That her children might get stolen, kidnapped, taken to a place where death awaits just like at home. She gives one, only one, of her children to a friend to hold. Just to keep safe until they cross. But the port of entry works funny, and some people get in faster than others. Including her son. Including your child. He crosses without you and is taken into custody. And it has been months since you've seen him and you tell them he's yours but they insist on proof and you're in San Diego while he's in Chicago and you don't know if he has eaten or has clothes and you tell me in Spanish, when your real language is Creole, that you're to blame for this. If only you had more hands.

Her story is your story is our story. Every dream, every love, every hope: all originated from the pit of your soul. Which is the only real home country anyway.

I believe that. Enough to leave this place I hate and collect my spirit. At least one more time so I can return. At least enough so that I can be part of the uprising that ends this place. I want to hold signs and hear my voice loudly. Above the choking whiteness. Because I understand more than ever that my liberation is intrinsically tied to yours. It is tied to everyone in every cage. It is tied to everyone who cannot breathe. There is no other choice for me anymore. It is all of us or none of us. If we cannot dream now of a world without cages, when will we?

It is a different world now for those inside that prison. I no longer sit with them in the suffocating room. I must listen to stories over scratchy telephone wires, entering my ear and making home inside my brain. I am never rid of the stories. They ring in my head like church bells. I hear from one woman, another, another. All telling me that they are forced to sign a liability waiver that states they will get a mask if they agree never to sue CCA when they catch the virus, if they die. When they refuse, they are pepper sprayed and placed in solitary confinement. They are not given masks. Two weeks later many of them are sick. They have fevers that make them delirious, aches that match their sorrow. I am forced to file against the facility. Forcing them to release these women because even after all this, even after, they still do not want to set them free. In a surprise turn of fate, the government agrees to release them. It is not because they have seen goodness, it is because they are afraid of the bad publicity these cases will cause. Similar to a case filed previously, that hit the news, where the government attorney admitted that the detainee was going to die and the only thing to do was offer "thoughts and prayers" to his family. I have never experienced such rage. Because the stories, they all live inside me now. Together and separately they make up who I am.

I think again of her, the last client I was able to see in person, the way she stared at me and told me, "I don't want to die." I wanted to tell her that she wouldn't. That I and all my degrees would win her case. That I am skilled. That I am the best attorney she could have asked for. The most hard-working. That I do not lose. That I will not lose her case. I open my mouth, but then shut it. Because although all those things are true, there is also a parallel truth. That I cannot guarantee anything. That I know not just the cards, but the whole house, is stacked against us. That in this jurisdiction there is an asylum grant rate of 13 percent by immigration judges. 13. The rest are denied and sent back to countries that can kill them. I can't promise you anything. Instead, I reach for my pendant and all my prayers to La Virgen return at once. And I say: "Your hair is soft silk. Your skin is the color of precious wet sand. I have memorized your face so that your children's children will know you."

And we breathe.

Briseida Salazar came to the United States from Michoacán, México when she was two years old. She is Elijah's mom, a DACA recipient, and she is currently in immigration proceedings. Since her experience in Otay Mesa Detention Center, she has decided to dedicate her life to fighting for social justice. At the time of writing her story, she was working three part-time jobs.

Briseida Salazar

No Lo Firmen! Don't Sign It!

April 8, 2020

I was locked up in Otay Mesa for a month and six days. I was scared of the virus that was taking over the world since the day I got to that place. All we knew was what was told to us, and the only ones telling us anything were the guards, the people I hated the most in this prison. The TVs in the dayroom were turned on the news channel all day. Sometimes it felt like the news was no help at all. The lady on the TV said the same thing over and over again. "Wear a mask. Practice social distancing. Wash your hands often." These things were impossible in a unit that held 128 women.

April 8, however, was exceptional. I woke up to all the girls in the unit whispering to each other. For a second, I was hoping it was good news, but from the look on their faces I knew it wasn't. Two girls had been taken out of our unit because they both had a fever. My fears became real as I read the paper on the window outside the unit. We were put on quarantine: no going out for chow, no visits to the law library, no visitations, no court appearances. This sucked. I couldn't take my mind off the fact that I would be stuck doing nothing, not that there was much to do in the first place, but I liked going to the library. Putting my nose in a book made me forget about the place I was stuck in. The library was our escape. For me it was a mental escape, but for most of the girls, it was their only way out. Attorneys were expensive and pro bono attorneys have a buttload of cases already, so most of the girls represented themselves in court. The law library was the only way they could win their case.

Later that day, I noticed almost no one wanted to leave their cell. It was odd. Usually the dayroom is full and loud. I realized everyone was afraid to be close to someone that might have the virus.

I was afraid and furious at the same time, and my best friend, Mary, felt the same way. So, we decided that we didn't care if we got into trouble. We would make a face mask. Vero joined in after we made ours, and pretty soon almost all of the girls wanted one too. We made the masks out of T-shirts, with hair ties for the ear loops and pantiliners as filters. We used whatever we could find. Eventually, we made more than 65 masks for the whole pod.

April 10, 2020

"I understand and agree to release and hold CoreCivic[1] and its agents and employees harmless from any and all claims that I may have related directly to my wearing the face mask."

When I read these words in the contract, I looked up at Irena, one of my cellies. She and I were two of the few girls in the whole pod who spoke English.

"Irena, we can't sign this." I said. She looked up at me very quickly as she finished reading the contract that had just been handed to us.

"This isn't right. No lo firmen!" she responded.

The rest of the girls in our cell looked confused. We all popped our heads out of our cells. When I spotted my friend, Patty, across the hall, I signaled to her not to sign the contract. She also spoke English, "No lo firmen!" she shouted to her cellies.

Patty grew up in a rough neighborhood in San Diego just like me, and Irena grew up in LA. Our whole lives we'd seen injustices happen to our people, and this was one more to add to the list.

CoreCivic, formerly the Corrections Corporation of America (CCA), is a company that owns and manages private prisons and detention centers.

"No lo firmen!" was yelled across the whole pod. Most of the women in the pod didn't understand what was going on. As A-Pod got louder and louder, Ms. Torres, the unit manager, became aware of the situation.

"If you are not going to sign it, I will be picking them up one by one. Si no lo van a firmar, los voy a recoger!" Ms. Torres yelled.

Irena responded so fast, "Translate the contract for the rest of the girls!"

Ms. Torres began to translate the contract out loud in Spanish, but she skipped over the most important part. She never mentioned that Core-Civic wouldn't be responsible if we got sick, or if anything happened to us during the pandemic. CoreCivic had found a way to protect itself against future lawsuits that were coming their way. In Spanish there's a saying, "Querían tapar el sol con un dedo," meaning they were basically trying to cover their ass. What bothered me most was that we were in a unit specifically for ICE—that meant that the majority of the detainees didn't speak or understand any English. In some cases, they didn't even speak Spanish. CoreCivic took advantage of this communication problem. They had all of the resources available to print the contracts in each and every language, but they tried to trick us and violate our rights in hopes that we were so scared of this virus that we would just give in.

Situations like this happened a lot in private for-profit detention centers where almost nobody had committed a crime, much less been convicted of one. Most of the women I was detained with ran from countries that raped them of their rights to live. The girls told me stories of bravery, stories of sadness and tragedy. Most of the women were asking for asylum. They came to this country to escape persecution for their political and/or religious beliefs, and even for their sexual orientations. In my time at Otay Mesa, I learned that abuse comes in every shape and size. Almost all of us had been abused one way or another.

But, all CoreCivic cares about is money. The more people incarcerated, the more money it makes. Who would have thought that the "Land of the Free" isn't so free after all? I couldn't imagine being in the shoes of the rest of the girls. Not only did I speak English, but I was also aware that we all had rights in this country.

I knew I had to do something, so I signaled the girls in the cell next to mine not to sign. They were Chinese. I don't know how I did it, but they understood exactly what I meant. The pod began to get louder. I was on the top tier, in the first room Ms. Torres came to. I could see her face as she became angry at a situation she couldn't control. I saw her face turn bright red like a tomato, and I heard her tone of voice change completely. It was like we had challenged her authority. She must have felt threatened because she began to clinch her teeth as she spoke. I knew she was trying to keep her cool.

"Okay, ladies, please pass the flyer back to me," she said.

Irena was the first bunk in the corner.

"No, I have a right to keep this document," she insisted.

Ms. Torres snatched it out of her hand and proceeded to the next girl. I had hidden the contract in my bra prior to her arrival, so when she asked me to give it her, I simply replied, "I need to speak to my attorney about this document, so, no, I'm not going to give it back. I have every right to keep this contract." She was furious, because she quickly realized we were right.

"Fine, if you won't give me the paper, you will be getting a write-up."

In most prisons a write-up doesn't mean shit to the inmates, but it was different for us; every write-up was a statement about your character in immigration court. Every "bad" thing you did inside the prison followed you throughout your case. For a moment, I thought about giving the stupid piece of paper back. I had so much waiting for me on the outs, I couldn't risk getting my bail refused, but I knew this was bigger than me and more than just my bail. This was about doing what's right, so I just bit my tongue as I watched her walk out of our cell.

Amid all the yelling, I heard her speak into her walkie-talkie: "I need back up now! Send the Emergency Response Team to Alpha now!"

In the blink of an eye, I saw men storm our pod. They were just the regular guards that are usually in the hallway coordinating where every-body goes, keeping the men and women separate and things like that. But now, they came in with only pepper spray. These kids, with the over-whelming responsibility of controlling the whole pod, were extremely young.

I watched Ms. Torres point out Patty as the head of the herd. She instructed her to come downstairs. As I saw Patty walk down the stairs, something came over me and without thinking, I followed her, along with five or six other girls. By the time she made it to the bottom, Patty had about ten of us surrounding her, preventing the guards from touch-ing her.

The guards circulated around us, pointing pepper spray. I was so scared, but my anger took over any fear I had, and I stood tall as I told Ms. Torres, "If Patty is punished, then we should all be punished."

She instructed us all to go back to our cells, including Patty. We all went upstairs, and Irena yelled at me to go back into my room. (I had a lot of respect for Irena. She was the first person in CoreCivic to show me kindness. The moment I walked into our cell, she gave me a bowl, a spoon with someone else's name carved on it, some noodles, and a few other things from her commissary, stuff that was super-expensive to buy in detention. I know it wasn't much, but it was weeks before my money would show up in my books.)

Only one other lady walked into Patty's cell to support her; she was an older lady. Seconds later I saw the guard escort the two of them out of the cell in handcuffs and take them downstairs. I knew they were going to the hole. It was forbidden for us to be in a cell that didn't correspond to us.

They took a total of three girls out of our pod and took them to the "hole," as we called it. Solitary. It's the worst place you want to be in a prison like this one. They strip you down to your underwear and bra and put you in a cell by yourself with nothing but a mattress and a toilet. You're in that cell for 23 hours of the day. You eat, sleep, and shit in that damn cell for however long your punishment is, only coming out for a shower. They strip every inch of dignity you have left. No commissary or phone calls home, not even a book to read. I've never been in the hole, but I've been told that the toilet is a hole in the floor. I swear, people must go crazy in there.

At one point one of the many inexperienced, and probably nervous, younger guards accidentally sprayed the bottom tier with pepper spray as he took it out of his belt. I heard someone yelling louder than anyone else.

"Nos están echando gas pimienta!!"

I could hear the girls downstairs coughing, but I was way too focused on Patty at that moment that I didn't know what had happened. I looked over the railing and connected eyes with my friend, Vero, who was on a legal phone call with her lawyers. I also watched her as she secretly hung up the phone and dialed a different number. Later I found out she was on a recorded call with a member of Pueblos Sin Fronteras, an organization that fights for immigration rights. They had recorded everything.

Moments after everything had happened, the guards delivered lunch to our pod.

We refused to eat until our friends got brought back. I wasn't hungry at all, but there were many ladies with medical problems who needed lunch but also refused. I watched as A Pod became more than just a unit. We had become sisters, we stood together, and there was unity for once in the whole pod. Usually, there are a lot of petty problems between the girls, mostly because of our different cultural backgrounds. Girls would fight over dumb shit like TV channels or microwave lines.

Everything changed that day. You could feel the tension in the pod. I was afraid for Patty because she suffered from depression and had been diagnosed with a tumor in her brain. I knew she wouldn't hold up in solitary for long. I remember calling my mother and sobbing about what had just happened. I was afraid for my life.

All I could think about was my two-year-old son. My mother told me she was out of work because she had a common cold so, because of COVID-19, she was instructed to stay home. My mother was responsible for my son since my son's father was also incarcerated in a jail only miles away from where I was. He was serving nine months in a county jail. What would happen to my son? Would I get out to see my mother one last time? Would I even make it out alive? After a couple hours we saw Ms. Torres walk into our pod and announce that they had thrown the documents away, and all we had had initially was a piece of paper with our pictures on it that signified that we had received the mask.

I wasn't satisfied yet. I was still shaking from the events that had just happened. But soon all of that would go away when I saw Patty and the two other girls walk back into our pod. Happy yells and whistles took over our pod as they stepped back into the place we now called home.

Later that night I decided to call Pueblos Sin Fronteras, and they gave me the phone number of a local newspaper, which gave me a chance to get our story out. When I called, the reporter on the other end of the line was friendly and seemed to genuinely care about our situation. When I told her what had happened, her tone of voice changed completely as she informed me that CoreCivic had reached out as well. She stated that CoreCivic told the media we were receiving masks that day but nothing about the contract. CoreCivic felt pressured.

The next day I woke up for chow at about five in the morning. I was brushing my teeth when I heard a familiar voice on the TV in the background. "¡Nos están echando gas pimienta!" It was the recording Pueblos Sin Fronteras had from when Vero had called them! They had sent it to the local news. It was all over the news the whole day. We had beat CoreCivic at its own game, but my fight wasn't over yet.

April 16, 2020

I had been tossing and turning all night, because I couldn't stop thinking about my bail court. I was being represented by a pro bono attorney from the Jewish Family Services. My mom had done everything to get me this attorney. She had no money for a paid attorney, and I was a single mother with no savings account. I was extremely nervous because my attorney was free, and I didn't know how serious they actually took their cases. I guess I thought they were just completing volunteer hours or some shit like that. I woke up early even though I knew I wasn't going to be taken to court. I picked up the phone and called my attorney. The machine on the other line began to speak, and I quickly hung up the phone. There was no point in waiting to leave a message. They knew who was calling and why. I immediately called my mom.

"¿Mom, qué pasó con la corte? Luis no me contesta." I asked because I didn't know what had happened in court.

"¿De verdad, no sabes qué pasó?" she responded. She thought I knew what had happened.

"No, Mom what happened?" I said.

"Sí, te la dieron!" she yelled with cheer.

"No! ¿Es en serio?" I said as I turned around and yelled, "Irena, I got my bail!" She was waiting to go into the shower next to the telephone where I was.

"Mom, how much is my bail?" I asked. When she answered that my $5,000 bail was being taken care of, she took advantage of the moment to remind me of my blessings and to tell me I needed to turn my life around.

"$5,000, pero la oficina de Luis los va a donar!" She told me that Luis's office was going to donate the money for my bail, and then she added:

"Mami es tiempo de que cambies tu vida y seas una mujer mejor porque mira todas las bendiciones que Dios te ha dado." She assured me that I had received many blessings and that I should turn my life around.

What my mother said that day really stuck with me. I used to think that my color and my roots were a curse, but today I know that my color and my roots are a blessing. I hope to be part of the change in our "justice" system, but it doesn't take one brown girl with big dreams. It takes a whole village.

Ismahan Abdullahi is a community organizer and racial justice and human rights advocate who is committed to justice and equity. She currently serves as the Executive Director of the Muslim American Society: Public Affairs and Civic Engagement. As she sat down to write her story, she kept thinking *survival, faith, resiliency.*

Ismahan Abdullahi

They Will Not Forget

I turn on the lights and walk to the restroom, every step feeling like a promise of a new day, a renewed sense of hope. My body shudders from the cold water I splash on my face as I make wudu, preparing for prayer. You should have waited for the water to warm up, I silently laugh to myself, but knowing deep down I wouldn't waste a single drop of water. Grateful to have running water, I begin the ritual washing. I wash my hands and arms, letting water run in between my fingers. I tilt my head back, glossing my wet hands over my hair and ears. I lift my right foot, then my left foot and wash them ceremoniously, remembering the numerous times I had to do this in a public bathroom. The strange glances and side-eye given by complete strangers wondering why I had my foot in the sink of a public bathroom. My unapologetic shrug as I focused on me and what I got to do. But in this quiet moment, it's as if the world stands still. My heart beats excitedly in anticipation of the morning prayer. That feeling of being able to throw the world behind your back for a few minutes, eliminating the loud noises, the burdens we shoulder, the uncertainty of tomorrow. Leaning into the Light that guides me and gives me strength. Nothing seems as certain as that moment that I stand in front of Allah.

"Bismillahi Rahmani Rahmiim…Alhamdulilahi Rabbil Alamin. Ar-Rahmani Rahiim, Maliki Youmi Deen," the first few verses of Surah Al-Fatiha roll off my tongue like a coursing river, reminding me of my beginning, my eternal destination, and centering my purpose. I cling to prayer deeply, like one who is desperate to breathe, gulping air fast and furiously. Prayer is my lifeline, my connection to the Eternal.

I sit there after completing my morning prayer, engaged in remembrance. I find the strength to get up. The day awaits…Bismillah.…

La Mesa

I got the call at 1:48 PM.

"Ismahan, help! I have tear-gas in my eyes," Sumaya blurted, her voice shaking with fear and pain. "We were protesting and the next thing we knew, they were shooting tear-gas at us!" Sumaya cried over and over again.

"We can't find Naima. We all got separated somehow," she said. My heart started to beat fast. I was in the middle of a strategy meeting when I received the call from Sumaya.

I was hoping to go to the protest at 3:00 PM, once my meetings were done, but I couldn't concentrate anymore. Not when Sumaya and the young people were being tear-gassed. I exited the Zoom meeting and closed my laptop, feeling like my heart was in my throat. Thankfully, I was dressed, and quickly grabbed a mask and my shoes. I wasn't too far from the protest. I prayed that I got there in time, unsure of what I would find when I arrived.

"Hang on, I'm coming," I told Sumaya. I instructed her to try to regroup with everyone at the Chevron gas station nearby.

Driving to La Mesa, I prayed silently. As I tried to reach the gas station that the youth were at, I saw complete chaos. People running everywhere, cars jam-packed on the street as if this were rush hour time on the Interstate 405 in Los Angeles. I drove around in circles trying to get to the gas station, frustrated that I couldn't get past the intersection of Broadway with a small cross street. There were shards of glass all over the sidewalk near the police station. The cars were not moving at all since there was a mass of people crossing the street in every direction. I finally was able to get closer to the intersection that I needed to cross. All I had to do was turn right next to the police station. There were only three cars ahead of me. Thank God, I thought. I'm so close.

"Ismahan, watch out!" yelled someone who I couldn't identify at first.

I stopped and looked around. My glance fell on a young man with a mask, yelling from across the street. He screamed at me to be careful, that what looked like snipers on the roof of the police station were shooting at cars passing that way with something he couldn't identify. I looked up horrified, and I felt the adrenaline kick in. I couldn't turn right anymore without putting myself in harm's way, but I had to get to the youth, and this was my chance to cross the intersection. I took a deep breath and prayed to Allah to keep me safe. There was only one car in front of me—I was almost there, so close, the traffic light turned green, and for a brief moment, there was no one crossing the street. The car in front of me turned right and I quickly followed before circumstances changed. I'm free. Alhamdulilah, I crossed the intersection, moving away from the police snipers. I found a place to park my car, and got out to find our group.

First, I heard screams. Then I saw smoke. People ran in multiple directions. I looked out in horror as people of every age ran into oncoming traffic, away from the smoke. Is that the tear-gas? There is no way this could be San Diego, I thought. There is no way this can be happening here. Tear-gas and rubber bullets here in La Mesa?

In the midst of a global pandemic that affected the respiratory system, the police deployed tear-gas against the people!

BANG!

"Where is Amina! What happened to Omar?" I screamed. I ran into Mejgan who came to aid me. We both looked at each other and understood what we had to do. We took a deep steadying breath and ran towards the crowd that had just been tear-gassed. We crossed the street, hoping to find Amina, Omar, and the rest of our young people who had gotten separated.

BANG! BANG!

A loud voice rang from above us:

"This is an unlawful assembly. You must disperse immediately."

The announcement came from a helicopter surrounding those who were protesting the injustice of brother George Floyd's death by cop. Unlawful? I looked around me, witnessing the sea of law enforcement with riot gear on, weapons pointed at unarmed protestors.

"Black Lives Matter! Know Justice! Know Peace! No Justice! No Peace!"

The chants grew louder as people rushed into formation, coming back to the parking lot as the tear-gas cleared. I watched the chaos around me, dismayed yet not surprised that those meant to "serve and protect" turned their weapons against unarmed protestors. There were people singing songs, waving signs, and honking cars. Music blared from cars parked along the streets.

In the middle of all this, an elderly lady, 60 to 65 in age, asked me how she could get to Sharp Grossmont Hospital because someone she knew had been hit in the head with a rubber bullet and had been taken to the hospital.

"Can you please tell me how I can get to Sharp Grossmont? What streets do we take?" She asked me this in such a soft voice, both steady and comforting.

"The police closed the entrance to the freeway here. Your best bet is to get to University Avenue and get to Fletcher Parkway or El Cajon Boulevard to take the 8 East from a different street," I told her.

The majority of the roads were blocked. The police encircled the crowd. A young 11-year-old boy standing near his mother cried as the tear-gas stung his eyes. I saw Mejgan trying to help pour water—or was it milk? the day was a daze—over his eyes, gently telling him how this would help him. I shook my head.

Somalia

BANG!

"They're coming!" someone screamed. Shots were fired. All I could see was fear in the eyes of the other refugees around me, feet flying in every direction.

"What's going on? May Allah protect us!" someone cried out.

One moment, we are sitting around in peace, eating our meal and enjoying each other's company. The next moment, our makeshift home—a small respite, a place to relax before we were to resume our journey to a refugee camp in Kenya—is bombarded by a raid from folks we couldn't identify. We were all seeking safety, running from the civil war that had broken our country. We stayed together, hoping to find safety in numbers. I remember the hard, brown sand with little to no vegetation, the scorching sun beating down on our backs. I played with small pebbles on the ground, sitting near my mother before the shots began.

"Run! Everyone. Run for cover. Get to the cars!" yelled out some men who started to grab anything they could use as shields to protect us. My mother hunched her body over my baby brother, protecting him from the bullets with her own body.

"Get up, we must get to the cars. Now. It's our only way to safety." I looked out in fear, unsure of what was happening. Was I going to lose my mother and family like I had lost my father? Maybe, if I ran, they would leave my momma alone. Afraid and unsure, I started running, my mother screaming my name behind me. Run. Survive. Protect. Before I could get far, my grandmother's warm hands picked me up and swung me on her hip. The look of anguish on her face broke me to pieces. Did someone die? My young eyes widened in shock, as I realized I had been placed in a car next to my mother.

"Momma!" I cried out in joy, tears running down my cheeks. I clung to her desperately, never wanting to let go.

"I don't want to lose you Momma. Let them get me, not you."

La Mesa

"Ismahan, Walid got hit! He's bleeding!"

BANG! BANG!

I didn't have time to think, to slow down or remember. I fought off the images of war, of pain that rushed through my mind. I swallowed the memories back, telling myself, "Not now, you can't remember the civil war now. You have to protect the young ones. Get them out of here now." I turned to Mejgan,

"We have to find them."

As I rushed back into the fray, gasping for air, because my lungs felt like they were on fire from the tear-gas, the terror of war surged through my body and brain again: Walid is hurt. We must find him. He's bleeding.

The tear-gas came out of nowhere this time, filling the air around us. I still hadn't found Walid, but now I had to run. I screamed out Walid's name and tried to keep an eye out for the others in the group around me. They were so young, so passionate, so determined. They shouldn't be experiencing this warfare.

"Here, pour water on your eyes. It'll help," I told the people around me, all of us still in shock at the amount of tear-gas we had just gotten hit with. I poured water over my eyes and the eyes of those around me, eyes that stung because of the tear-gas. Our own government had just used chemical warfare against us. I was swept away by the torrents of life in that instant. Juggling and thrashing me against memories of escaping Somalia. I tried to hang on to this moment, pushing the memories back.

"Ismahan, we found him! He's here. A medic tended to him already. Thank God," Mejgan exclaimed, breaking me out of my daze.

We found Walid. He was bleeding profusely, but a medic had tended to him. He had been shot multiple times with rubber bullets. As we assessed his injury, asking him to go to the hospital, another round of tear-gas was deployed near us. We had to run again. To survive. To protect.

"The National Guard is on the way!" someone shouted. Multiple law enforcement agencies were coming. They were closing in. We had to get out. Walid needed medical attention.

Somalia

It would be years later in my adult life that I learned that look of anguish on my grandmother's face that fateful day. Little did I know that as I had run away during that chaotic moment, my youngest aunt had run as well. She had run in the opposite direction from me. My grandmother had seen us both running. She understood she couldn't save us both, and in that split second she had decided to save me because she couldn't bear the thought of her daughter losing her child.

"In aa gabadhaya waayo aya ii dhaamto in ee hooyada ku waayi lahed," *I'd rather lose my own daughter and bear the pain than have your mother go through that anguish.*

Allah was looking out for us, for a kind stranger found my aunt and brought her to our car that fateful day. Till this day, we say that Allah rewarded our grandmother for her sacrifice by making sure my aunt stayed safe and in the same car that we were all in. My grandmother's cry of pain turned to a cry of gratitude.

"Alhamdulilah, all praise is to Allah," she repeated.

La Mesa

The noise grew louder. More and more folks were coming to the area to protest, and law enforcement numbers were increasing.

"Look! White supremacists are here," Mejgan said as she pointed to a man filming people. I took note of his car, plastered with hateful messages of intolerance.

"We have to leave now, before things escalate further," I said. Mejgan and I made sure the youth left, giving the ones with no rides a lift.

I looked at the clock in the car. It read 8:54 PM. I felt drained, exhausted yet grateful that we were all alive. The young ones were safe. I was safe. For now.

The drive home was long and hard. Alone with my thoughts, I reflected on the day's action. I was left with myself and reflections of forgotten memories. Allah, Allah! The gentle morning had turned into a whirling gale. Who could've known what the day would hold? Reliving the memories of the civil war made me sad that this generation had to experience what they had experienced in La Mesa that day. It's a moment in time they will not forget.

We can't change the past. But we will fight for the future. Our lives depend on it. Faith, strength, resiliency. The world should never underestimate us.

Tomorrow I will I sit after completing my morning prayer, engaged in remembrance. And I will find the strength to get up, because the day awaits.... Bismillah.... Inhale, exhale, breathe.

Missy Solis is a librarian from La Mesa, California.

Missy Solis

Dispatches from La Mesa

August

I am writing this from La Mesa, California. It is summertime during a global pandemic. In California, grief is everywhere and nowhere at the same time. The loneliness drifts in and out. I think of the flowers that bloomed this spring, how they would sing to me as I walked through the neighborhood.

April

At first, I took solace in daily walks through the neighborhood. I discovered secret staircases and walkways. I felt a kinship with a neighbor dressed in an astronaut suit and tried to think of my own disguise. Once, I marveled at a basket of fresh oranges sitting on someone's lawn. A sign on the basket said, *Take as many as you like.*

The hills I walk each day lead me past the same house with a giant stuffed teddy bear sitting on a bench. I take comfort in that sad, old bear—how it droops like a drunkard and no one cares to remove it. Sometimes when I am out on a walk, I lower my pandemic mask to smell a rose in someone's yard. All the roses here are like the kind you see at funerals or sold on the side of the road. Still, I feel humbled to watch them bloom in pinks and oranges.

Children are nowhere, but all over the sidewalk I see messages scrawled in pastel-colored chalk. *Strong, calm, happy, isolate* is written on four different steps that lead up to someone's house.

Most days I walk up and down the same hills and arrive back at home about forty-five minutes later, confused as to if I've just experienced anything new at all. One day, a bird on a telephone pole nearly shits on me. I laugh to myself.

Michelle and Celeste

Two days into the stay-at-home order I drive to my sister Michelle's house at two in the morning to deliver a thermometer. She is convinced that she has contracted COVID-19 from her roommates—one a social worker, another a Home Depot handyman. Michelle has a severe case of asthma and a five-year-old daughter named Celeste.

When the pandemic began, I thought about how the workers in my family would be required to stay on the job, despite all the risks. So much depends upon what we all do. A custodian, two grocery store workers, two public school teachers, a librarian.

In March I find myself working from home and in a constant state of worry. About my mother in a rural community, scrubbing toilets in an empty school. About my teenage niece and my brother, essential workers at the same Vons grocery store in El Cajon, where the cases are always higher.

Mindy

My twin sister and I celebrated our 36th birthday in March, just days after the stay-at-home order was issued in California. Mindy currently lives in a small town called Tivoli—over three thousand miles away in upstate New York. In the pond outside Mindy's rented house, the reflection of a giant willow tree materializes at just the right times of day.

I envy her closeness to nature as I sit in air conditioning and look at the crispy palm tree outside my window. The tree is suffering. I see its sagging fronds and think, Maybe this is one way to describe how we all feel right now.

Mindy does not like videoconferencing. "I don't want to be on the screen," she says when I try to put together a Zoom call with friends. We do it anyway, and it is a small comfort, like a new bloom on a neighborhood cactus.

May 30, 2020

On May 25th, a familiar wave of grief ripples through America after a Black man named George Floyd is murdered in broad daylight by the police in Minneapolis, Minnesota. People take to the streets all across the country in protest, this time covered in masks to prevent the spread of COVID-19. A police station in Minneapolis is burned to the ground. The grief is everywhere—everywhere in the repetition of senseless harm, year after year. And yet for some, the symbolism does not register.

Two days after Floyd is killed, cell phone footage surfaces that shows a young man named Amaurie Johnson harassed by the La Mesa Police while he is waiting outside an apartment complex for a friend. In the video, he asks why he is being approached. What has he done? The question sits heavy in the air.

It's Saturday. Michelle pushes Celeste in a stroller as we walk from her apartment towards the parking lot of the La Mesa Police Department. People from La Mesa and throughout San Diego County have arrived to participate in a protest against police brutality and racism. They carry signs with the names of the dead: Breonna Taylor, Ahmad Arbery, George Floyd. They carry signs that demand justice for our neighbor Amaurie Johnson, arrested for no reason and pushed around by a police officer who had no regard for him.

I throw my homemade sign in the stroller and pull it out once we arrive at the parking lot, where hundreds have gathered to protest. Michelle stays in the back of the crowd, and when the march begins, we

s hot out and Celeste needs a nap. As we march from Alli-
... Avenue towards University, a man plays a trumpet on the median.
For the first time in a long time, there is some relief to be found in the
sound of our voices together.

May 31, 2020

Last night the La Mesa Police used chemical agents and "bean bag"
rounds on people who had gathered to peacefully protest. Last night a
grandmother named Leslie Furcron was shot in the face by the La Mesa
Police and remains in critical condition.

I walked from the protest to my sister's apartment in the late afternoon—and on the way I saw the San Diego Sheriff pull into a secure
parking lot of the La Mesa Police Department. The police were deco-
rated in excessive riot gear and seemed poised to end the demonstration
in any way they deemed necessary.

The jewel of the hills is tarnished, and perhaps it has always been so.

Denial

The morning after the protest, Michelle pushes Celeste in her stroller
as we walk around picking up trash in the neighborhood. Outside the
still-burning Chase bank, an old white man in a Trump T-shirt loudly
says that he has the right to shoot the fuckers who did this.

In downtown La Mesa I see a tiny Boy Scout scrubbing George
Floyd's name off the sidewalk and wonder what his parents have told
him about what occurred here. I wonder if they have told him anything
about George Floyd and the police who killed him.

In the days following the protest, strange white men in neon vests
take it upon themselves to patrol the downtown La Mesa area and its
businesses. No one has requested their help. No one is seeking their protection.

LA MESA STRONG banners pop up all across the city, shouting in capital blue letters.

Every time I see one, I think: What if we could be vulnerable and own up to our wrongs? What if we could learn how to make amends? Here in La Mesa we still don't understand grief. Whatever strength there is to find in this community—it is going to take a long time to realize.

Growing up, **Zack** was surrounded by skateboarding and punk rock. He was at a Black Flag (famous punk band) show at five months old and, with a complicated upbringing, attended different schools nearly every year or two. Zack naturally drifted toward the skateboarding culture like his father did, where he would learn from and meet lifelong friends.

Zack Dowdy
Rolling for Rights

I'm a San Diego native born at the El Cajon hospital in 1987. Today, I'm 33 years old. I went to four different high schools, and can't remember all the elementary or middle schools I attended. To say the least, my environment changed constantly while I was growing up. But I was always around skateboards and punk rock culture. My dad was a skateboarder; he sold skateboard trucks to pay for my diapers.

I have a hard time finding the exact moment skateboarding clicked and became my entire world. I was 15 years old when my dad took me on a road trip to a skateboard contest at an empty pool that was so far away—it seemed like travelling to another country. My friends, Josh and Terry, were so excited on the drive, talking about which skaters they were looking forward to seeing at the contest, as we all were mesmerized by the mountains and empty, deserted landscape in route to this empty pool where the contest was taking place. I will never forget the day we finally pulled off the long I-15 stretch and arrived at a dirt road that wrapped around an abandoned house with hundreds of parked cars. The energy of this event felt so authentic, everyone screaming, encouraging one another. It was like electricity moving through every single body standing and sitting around this empty pool, feeding off each other's blood, sweat, and laughter. This event was a fundraiser for a professional skateboarder who was wrongfully arrested, the same skateboarder who taught me how to "drop in" on mini-ramps only a few years earlier at Contraband Skate Shop in Downtown San Diego.

I was 17 when I moved out of my mother's house and started to build my own foundation. I decided to start a zine called *Typical Culture*. The ideology behind creating a zine was to give the underground San Diego skate community a platform to build on, without the control or manipulation of the politics of the skateboarding industry. About one year into *Typical Culture*, I was already holding events with hundreds of skateboarders, organizing skateboard contests, fundraisers, and video premiers. A lot of this happened naturally, which eventually led me to landing a job with some of the world's best-known skateboard journalists, Grant Brittain, Dave Swift, and others. In 2019 I decided to put down the torch of *Typical Culture*. It had been such an amazing time in my life, but I didn't want to drag it out too long. I wanted to look back and appreciate it. On a high note. I was ready for some change, not knowing where or what the change was, but I was ready.

It was May 30th, 2020, just days after a young Black man was wrongfully arrested at the La Mesa trolley stop. That's when I walked onto the 8 East freeway with my fiancé, protesting for justice with hundreds of other San Diegans in the middle of a global pandemic, demanding justice for George Floyd, Breonna Taylor, and the countless other lives taken at the hands of police officers. Later that afternoon, the protest ended at the La Mesa Police Department. A long day that ended with me and my fiancé teargassed, running from the large smoke clouds, and pouring milk on each other's eyes. I asked myself, what is my role in this? I'm not comfortable sitting back and watching my community get trampled on. They can knock us down tonight, but I'll come back harder than before. It was a moment of one of those realizations when one discovers that the action that needs to be taken isn't going to be easy, but it's necessary for change. Skateboarding taught me that at a young age.

The next morning, I found myself stumped on finding my role. As a white male I'm naturally affiliated with the oppressor and the oppression that I'm very much trying to dismantle. "How do I make a stand?" I realize I'll never experience the struggles and injustices that I'm fighting against. But I remembered a few specific moments that suddenly came to my mind, one of which was my dinner at my friends Terry and Derral Hamilton's house. I remember how much love was in that house—there was so much passion. At that dinner, I realized that an important connection I had with all of these friends was skateboarding—it was right in front of me. This was our shared lane to make a stand.

I called my Black skateboard friends for their input. First was Tyrone Olson, a skateboarding legend who's really made a footprint on San Diego skateboarding.

"What do you think about a skateboard protest? We can roll in solidarity for all the Black and Brown lives taken by police brutality." Tyrone's reaction wasn't a yes or no, it was already something he'd been trying to figure out.

Then I called Shuriken (Shannon) to see if he was on board. Same thing. He wanted to make a stand but wasn't sure how. Lastly, I called Brandon Turner, a Black pro skateboarder who had been a victim of the systemic issues we're fighting. From prisoner to rehab instructor, his involvement really lit my fire. Like many important moments in my life, I realized that unless I opened the door, I would never know what's on the other side. These were my friends, and they were also respected professional skateboarders, and together we would plan to organize an action that would roll in the face of injustice.

Less than two weeks before the event, we utilized our platforms as skateboarders to spread the word. I was in shock, and also grateful, to have assembled San Diego's professional skateboarders: Brandon Turner, Shuriken Shannon, Tommy Sandoval, and Tyrone Olson for this movement. Before we made any announcements, I created an Instagram account specifically for this event so anyone interested could gain more insight into the Rolling for Rights action. Between the four of us, we had 196,000 followers on Instagram, so that was where we started to spread awareness. We planned to post everything at once, with the objective of making a big splash in our community in order to catch the attention of as many skateboarders as we could. The effort worked. Our community of skaters started reposting the event. Skate shops got behind it. Some of the largest publications in skateboarding, including *Transworld Skateboarding*, promoted the event for us. It was like wildfire spreading through the skate community.

Then I received a voicemail from a San Diego detective. I told everyone involved I would deal with it, because I didn't want that responsibility pinned on them. In my head I repeated: The event is happening. I'm not going to cancel or let this detective scare us. I walked around my block every 30 minutes for three days straight because my mind was racing; I've learned over time that if I'm physically able to move my body, I tend to find a better place of mental stability. Walking down a quiet neighborhood road, I decided to call the San Diego detective back, but he didn't answer, so I left a professional voicemail. Five minutes later I received a text from the detective's phone number that read, "Thank you."

That's it? Thank you? All that worry for nothing.

I will never forget June 20th, 2020. On that day, I solidified the skateboarding mindset I had made for myself. My life shifted. I felt validated—skateboarding was my purpose. I had begun skateboarding because it was fun and a way to hang out with kids in my neighborhood. In retrospect, it was a way to deal with a lot of dysfunctional family issues I had at home. That was common with my close friends as well. Skateboarding is fairly cheap, and lucky for me, my dad was a skateboarder.

I can't explain the feeling of rolling down Sixth Avenue with thousands of other skateboarders around me. I didn't just roll like most people. I pushed the entire 3.4 miles. In those moments, I reached another mental place, a form of meditation. It's really hard to describe the experience, but I do remember at one point rolling down Ash Street, waving my flag high with black letters that read "Rolling for Rights." I remember this specific moment because I finally looked up, and I snapped back to reality. I looked into the eyes of bystanders while rolling through an intersection near Little Italy with thousands of skateboarders around me. I've never felt so liberated. I remember the moment when I locked eyes on an older white man in a Porsche while pushing through that intersection. I raised my fist, and he nodded his head. I was so happy, because it was in that instant, I realized how powerful this was going to be. The man in the Porsche would have to face thousands more people that felt the same way I did, stuck in his car.

Rolling for Rights wasn't the first event I've organized, but it's the first one I'm extremely proud of because it was for a purpose so much more than just skateboarding. I'm happy to use skateboarding as an avenue to disrupt that barrier of entry to politics, because it wasn't until recently that I realized that's how we're going to change this broken system. I'm learning how to call in, not out. Much like learning a new trick, you can't force it upon yourself or anyone else. You have to fall, learn from your slam, and keep applying what you learn until you land it. The hard part is taking that leap past fear, taking the chance to fall. It doesn't mean that somebody can't give you tips based on their respective experiences, but it's also important to know everyone has their own process of learning and developing. Allowing them to go through that process gives them the feeling of success. That's been the real game changer. This event has made me a better person. I understand emotion better; I understand reactions better; I'm more practiced; I'm not so quick to judge; but most importantly, I feel like I have a real family and sense of community.

I want to share my passion for skateboarding with the next generation of youth who are diverse and might not quite see the connections between skateboarding and political action yet. We need to stand up and continue this current fight for racial justice in San Diego and around

America. While I'm writing this, we're planning our next event, because this movement isn't going to end anytime soon, and change will only come from momentum. One thing is for sure. The San Diego skate-boarding-for-social-justice community is alive and thriving.

Ana Laura Martinez grew up in a working-class and immigrant household in Tijuana and San Diego. She is a worker justice advocate, does mutual aid work, and is committed to envisioning different futures together.

Ana Laura Martinez

Compounded Fear

I remember it was a Monday. I needed to start my workday at 8:30 AM, and I had literally rolled out of bed at 8:28 AM, giving me a momentary illusion that I was running on time. Buuuuut, I *never* run on time, and I didn't that day.

I think it was around 3 PM when I got *the call*. It was from a friend I had physically distanced with a few days before. That outing was my first physical distancing gathering in weeks, and I was hella HYPED! I saw friends who I hadn't seen in some time—I shared space and laughter, and I heard their voices in person, and I caught up on the *chisme*, and it was a moment where I could just be, to be.

The fear of COVID-19 had kept me home (and still does!). My commitment to staying in place, guided by my fear, allowed me to intimately get to know the nooks and crannies of my home, of my room. So much so, I can tell you where the cobwebs I proudly accept reside, where the trail of ants starts and ends in my room, which floorboards creak the most (and which I sometimes purposely step on to hear the *creak, creak*), tell you of my favorite place to lay on the floor to get lost in thought, and tell you how the sunlight dances through my room from sunrise to sunset.

I had just wrapped up my fifth Zoom meeting when I took her call, and I was now in the kitchen, taking a break from washing dishes.

"Hey, what are you doing?" Her voice sounded down.

"Just working, what's up?" I responded.

"I need to tell you something. Don't freak out, okay?"

Had something happened to her? Since she's also my neighbor and lives less than a mile away, I was ready to bike over immediately if something was up. The tone in her voice made me walk from the kitchen to my room, to sit on my bed.

"Okay, what is it? What happened?"

"So...." Her voice was cracking, and it made me think that she might have been crying before the call. "I just learned that I spent time with a friend who came into contact with someone who tested positive for COVID-19. This happened before the gathering yesterday. If I had known, I wouldn't have gone. I'm sorry."

I felt so much in response to having been exposed to COVID-19: numbness, like I was no longer inhabiting my body, like I had something stuck in my throat. I don't know how to accurately describe the feeling I felt, but it was an immense feeling I have only felt two other times.

The first time was when I sat by my abuelita's hospital bed, holding her hand and seeing the signs of death manifest in her blue-grey fingers and her diminishing breath, fearing a world without her. Even though I had lived my entire 20 years of life with her, shared a bedroom with her, I felt regret for not loving her more, felt robbed at not having more time with her.

The second time was when I saw my dad pack his few belongings with such precision: his personal documents and photos from the last drawer of his dresser and his well-worn clothes from the closet. His departure made me fear a future without him, too. Would my mom be able to navigate her sadness? What would this mean for our father-daughter relationship? So much uncertainty.

Just like in both instances, I fell apart and sobbed. My friend continued talking about details, and I zoned out, falling into my bed, feeling this immense sense of fear, this impending sense of doom.

In between the crying I said, "I need to go process this...I am hanging up."

We all know that COVID-19 is an invasive and unpredictable disease, affecting one's lungs, brain, kidneys. It seems as time goes on we learn how it affects every aspect of your body.

Let me explain my fear of COVID-19. It is rooted in several things. The fear of infecting others, the fear of being a burden on my loved ones while sick, and the fear of dying from something this shitty country refuses to address seriously. If you Google COVID-19, you will read how it affects those with "underlying conditions the most," and you will read how a majority of deaths were because they had those "underlying conditions." This logic does not make me feel better; on the contrary, it is infuriating. I have seen this logic make people feel invincible and accept the twisted and ridiculous (but preventable) outcome that people with chronic illnesses and disabilities will die. This is ableism and fatphobia on full display during a global pandemic.

As a fat woman of color, I know my chances of surviving COVID-19 are slim because of how fatness is read in the medical industrial complex. In my early adulthood, I would go to the doctor for many things: a rash on my leg, a cough, or an alarming menstruation cycle. I was always told the same thing every time: Lose weight and all would be fine. WHAAAAAAAAAT? The actual symptoms I went in for were never addressed. The burden of having them treated always landed on me, and I was read as an insubordinate patient.

The fear of having been exposed to COVID-19 debilitated me. I spent the rest of the day crying in my room. I reflected on the last few days since the gathering. Had I interacted with anyone since then, had I put anyone at risk? I hadn't interacted with anyone except my roommate. I knew I had to tell her. It was my responsibility to do so. I rehearsed the conversation in my head a lot, and I disliked that I was having to do this. I regretted attending that physical distancing gathering, and I owned that I had made an irresponsible decision.

"Hey, I physically distanced with someone who came into contact with someone who tested positive for COVID-19. I know it sounds weird, but this shit is real, and COVID-19 is unpredictable, so I will be taking the necessary precautions to keep us safe, and I will quarantine in my room for the next two weeks."

After I told her, I immediately researched ways to get tested. Because I had no symptoms a few days after the gathering, Kaiser deemed me low-priority, and I couldn't get tested through them. The county hadn't moved to walk-ins at that point, and all testing centers required appointments. The earliest one I could get was that Saturday. On top of that, I was told that I wouldn't know the results for another three to five days. So, it would be eight to ten days before I would know my test results.

As a worker justice advocate, I thought of the many people who do not have the luxury to work from home and the many people who do not have the sick days necessary to take up to ten days to get their test results back. Or even the necessary days to allow for a safe and healthy quarantine, so they can ensure their safety and stop the spread of COVID-19. I thought of my older brother who is a trolley conductor, of his girlfriend who is a cashier at 7/11, of my former sister-in-law's partner who works at a car dealership, all of whom cannot work from home and face the fear every time they go back home from work. I couldn't help but wonder if I am bringing death into my home.

My personal fear was compounded with this grief, this heartbreak at how the state is continuing to uplift policies that are exacerbating the forms of violence against Blacks, people of color, immigrants, and poor people. Reopening the economy is coming at the expense of their deaths, because they are deemed exploitable and disposable.

The first few days had me spiral into a headspace where I was not doing well. My mental health was at its shittiest, and that moved my sister to ask me, "Do you have intentions to hurt yourself?" When she first asked the question, I couldn't confidently answer no. I just cried. This fear was debilitating. I disconnected, disengaged, and isolated myself.

Ten days later, however, I confirmed that I'd tested negative. Though I was relieved, this experience has drastically altered my behavior. Since then I have become even stricter in how I quarantine. Aside from my roommate, I only see my mom and sister. I don't go to stores. Everything is curbside pickup. I have rejected several invites to physical distance with friends who I love and miss dearly. If I accept, though, it is after ensuring it is a small group, a group that can confidently answer they haven't done anything to put themselves at risk.

A friend joked that gauging who to physical distance with is similar to the questions you pose for consensual sex: Who have you shared space with? Have you been wearing your mask? Since your last physical distancing with people outside of your household, how have you been feeling? Have you gotten tested?

I am still recuperating from those two weeks of heavy isolation. Some relationships have shifted, and I have 153 unread texts that I keep promising myself to go through, but haven't. But I am grounded in my work as an advocate and activist that another world is possible, even in these scarier times. As Mary-Wynne Ashford writes, "*We sustain each other in dark times, sometimes simply by being present together.*"

Ree Obaña was born in Skyline, San Diego and currently resides in Paradise Hills. She is a daughter to Filipino immigrants, a single mother, community organizer, and mental health licensed clinical social worker.

Ree Obaña

Living in the Time of COVID

I arrived home to an empty and quiet house. I didn't bother turning on the lights as I usually do. Instead, I found my way to my living room floor and took a seat. Leaned up against my couch, I sat in silence, staring down the hallway leading to my bedroom. I thought to myself, Perhaps I should start getting ready for bed, but for some reason, I could not bring myself to move. I just sat there, in the dark, in stillness, with my legs folded and hands gripped in my lap. My eyes felt heavy from the long day, and I found comfort in the low humming sound of the fridge and every tick-tock of the kitchen clock. The rhythm was nearly in sync with my own pulse, and it was guiding me into this meditative state, or at least that's what I had hoped. For many reasons, I just could not calm my thoughts and the worries I'd been preoccupied with lately.

My mind kept harassing me, pushing me to get up and, "Keep going!" But my body, it felt as though I was anchored to the ground and trapped. Not feeling in control catapulted me into this panic. I could feel my heartbeat in my hands, a bounding pulse. I knew what was happening and what had to happen next. "You need to breathe," I said out loud. I felt my chest getting tighter, and I was unable to take a full breath. "What if I'm having a heart attack? I don't want to die alone." I repeated the self-directive again, knowing I would stubbornly deny my own advice, "Take slow deep breaths through your nose." These were the very coping skills I would offer and encourage my own clients to use in order to help decrease stress and anxiety. And there I was, a clinician, battling myself in a moment when I was in need. I glanced at a framed photo on the wall of my daughter, Frankie Simone, and I had no choice but to surrender. A visual of her baby face always calms me and reminds me to refocus.

I closed my eyes and mouth, placed my left hand on my chest and my right hand on my stomach, slowly inhaling through my nose, allowing my belly to expand outward. Visualizing the moment that I first held Frankie Simone in my arms, a little life I had grown and held in my womb, it grounded me back to the power and strength I knew I encompassed. I exhaled, slowly feeling the air travel through my pursed lips, imagining all of the knots in my neck untangling and my fears and tension exiting my body. I repeated these breathing patterns a few more times, slow and smooth, and on my last exhale I was overcome with this feeling of vulnerability. My eyes began to well up with tears, and I began to cry. Hugging my knees to my chest, curled up into a ball, I released a cry that seemed like I had been storing it away since this pandemic struck us. "It's a lot," I cried. "It's just too much."

I had just come home from a funeral and celebration of life for our dear friend, who transitioned far too soon from this earth, away from his wife and their two babies. The sight of their seven-year-old-daughter crying in her mother's arms after the closing of his casket and saying goodbye will forever be imprinted in my mind. How can this be? This life that we expect to live and the milestones we hope to witness in our children's lives, suddenly gone. And, just as painful, our children in grief, accepting the loss of their own beloved parent.

I cried this night, thinking about my own mortality and that of my daughter. How much time do I *really* have? Have I been living my life in gratitude, appreciating and loving every moment? Am I doing my best to be present and supportive of my child, especially during these scary and unpredictable times? I felt a fear and an angst I could not explain but perhaps finally understood after all these years, as I reflected on my own mother's mothering. I now understood her every worry and effort to love us, protect us, and prepare us to survive on our own. I will never truly understand her journey to this country as an immigrant woman, but I am indebted to her sacrifice. After 46 years of serving her community as a registered nurse, this woman continues to work during the pandemic, risking her own health. I think about my sister, relatives, cousins, and the countless number of friends and colleagues who are also essential healthcare workers, armed and ready on the frontline fighting COVID-19, despite this government's inadequate support and supplies to them. They continue to show up and care for others, without bias and prejudice, despite the anti-Asian racism spewing from the 45th president of the United States of America.

In these tears I cried, there was also a burning rage that could not be contained. While my family and friends have grown weary and tired from working in COVID units, quarantined away from their own children, we witness Trump supporters and "protestors" rallying for their right to go to the beach and to golf. They protest against the order to shelter in place, refusing to wear a mask because this is just entirely too great of an inconvenience for them. Meanwhile, the number of nurses dying, many of them Filipino, continues to grow. The statistics began to show that the people who are actually dying in this global crisis are, indeed, the immunocompromised, Black and Brown communities that are already predisposed to health conditions like sickle cell or diabetes, putting them at much higher risk. They are the prisoners locked up in cages, the "undocumented" sitting in detention centers. How can society be so damn cold? How is human life and public health not a priority for everyone? And then, I remember the brazen history of this country and how we came to be on this Native land we occupy today. Freedom and safety are reserved only for a select few.

There were difficult discussions we had had with our own children, and it broke me to see my nieces and nephews in tears when we sat them down to finally have "the talk" with them. As Black/Filipino youth, their reality is daunting. As a mother, auntie, and mental health clinician, it angers my soul that this system forces us to take their innocence away when we have to teach them how to protect themselves from police and racists. It angers me that a white, privileged "family" member boldly cries out on social media about her rights being violated because she cannot run on the beach. Meanwhile, Black people in America risk their lives when going for a run, going to class, or sleeping.

From the time I began writing this piece, Black mothers continue to lose their children to the police state, civil rights leaders have passed on, and I have learned of the deaths of more friends and clients. I've attended virtual funerals and through a glass door said my last goodbyes to my uncle who was dying of terminal cancer. I learned that after 12 years of serving our veterans as a licensed clinical social worker, my job refuses to support me during this pandemic and accommodate my need to be here for my daughter as schools continue to be closed. I struggled deeply with putting all of this down on paper. I avoided every opportunity to write, because I knew it would mean having to confront feelings that I had intentionally tucked away in order to survive and function. In my line of work, we must be ready to absorb other people's emotions, trauma, stress, pain, and loss. And here I was, at capacity, as a single mom, organizer, clinician trying to figure out how to stay afloat while helping others. But then I am reminded, "What good are we to others and this movement if we cannot take care of ourselves?" So, here I write with hopes to heal and self-care. I write so my daughter can look back and remember this time in history where it all felt like "too much" to handle but we made it through, collectively.

Living in the time of COVID and uprisings has caused a seismic shift in the universe and in my own life. It has called on me to adapt, to make important life-changing decisions as a single mom, so that I may support my own child's mental health and well-being. It has magnified the need to practice mindfulness, to embrace and find joy in the "here and now." It has reminded me that even in the midst of chaos, loss, and unrest, how vital it is to find pockets of silence and solitude when I can. It is there that I can find answers and re-root myself to my inner strengths. It is there where I can find my pulse: to inhale and exhale, with continued hope for another day.

Leslie Furcron was born at Booth Memorial Hospital in Cleveland, Ohio. In 1986, she and her family moved to San Diego, California where she has spent most of her adult life and has often shone as the creator of fun and community among her friends and family. She has learned to make a lot out of a little and continues to spread love and light to everyone who crosses her path. Leslie is the mother of four children (three living) and 13 grandchildren. After being shot by a La Mesa police officer during a peaceful protest, she hopes to one day regain vision in her left eye. This is her story.

Leslie Furcron

Abdul Jabar Rajai Furcron, or Leslie's Story

On the night of May 30th, 2020, I found myself in critical condition and life-flighted from Grossmont Hospital to the ICU unit at Sharp Memorial.

Tired of being silent, that night I used my voice. I yelled, "murderers!" as loud as I could at a protest for justice, a protest for all of the lives lost by police and their blatant abuse of power. That evening, I was shot in the middle of my forehead with a "bean bag" that nearly killed me. The officer, Eric Knudsen, who shot me that night is good friends with the La Mesa chief of police (who recently announced his retirement), and they covered for him. That night, Officer Eric Knudsen didn't like my voice. He didn't like what we were saying, he didn't like what we represented, and he shot me.

But my nightmare didn't start there.

It was 1983, I was already a mother to two children, and I was living in Long Beach where I was enrolled at Long Beach City College studying to be a nutritionist. LA county during the 80s was the peak of the crack cocaine epidemic in Black communities (and now we know this was all with intention). I was always considered a social butterfly and kept the company of many friends. I enjoyed life, I enjoyed people, and I was the "life of the party."

So, I ran the streets, or rather, I let the streets run me.

It was the father of my children who introduced me to drugs. He would always find excuses to go do things alone in the room. I asked him what he was doing because that was our bedroom, and he'd just say, "Ain't none of your business what's going on!" He knew it wasn't good, because he was raised like me, and we weren't raised in families that would have been okay with that lifestyle. This is the power and control drugs had over us.

We had just had our son, who was nine months old. We had a new baby and were looking for intimacy and love in the wrong place. And it was at that time that he allowed me into that bedroom, and I began using drugs with him. Our apartment was on Pacific Coast highway and Atlantic Avenue. It was a one-bedroom apartment, and our room had a king-size bed.

The dresser is where everybody gathered to "free-base," or what we called "baseballing." Freebasing is when you get the powder formation and mix it with baking soda. There would be four or five of us in that room, and that bowl would have four or five stems sticking out from it. In 1984, I smoked through my entire pregnancy with my daughter. Luckily, the state didn't take kids at that time for that reason, because if it were today, my daughter would have surely been taken from me right after delivery. Thank God I missed that. The state never came for my children, but my mother saw my lifestyle and made the decision to take them from me.

My mom was a money-hungry enabler; she liked men and money! I never wanted to have relationships like my mom, or even be like my mom, but my life and relationships ended up more chaotic when the drugs got implemented. But I thank God for my mom! Through all of that, she still came and rescued my children. She came to me and said it just like this: "I really don't know what's going on with you, Leslie, but I see that there's a problem. But, Bitch, you don' lost your mind, and in the process of losing your mind, you gon' lose your children! So, they are coming with me."

She was also clear that she'd take my check every month to care for the children. My mother intervened, because she knew I would eventually get my kids taken from me. She knew I was not on top of my game. In the NA/AA Fellowship, a non-profit organization for recovering addicts, they would say: "We are going to love on you until you are able to love on yourself." I had stopped loving on myself, but my mom loved on me. She protected my children, but she couldn't protect us all.

◆ ◆ ◆

No mother ever wants to receive a call about the death of her child. On the night of February 11th, 2020 as I left my job site, I got a call from my daughter, and she told me that I needed to pull over. She told me that my son had been pulled over for a "broken tail light," which resulted in a high-speed chase by the police where he hit a tree at 100 miles per hour and died.

I'll back up a little and explain that my son was only 15 when he was tried as an adult and sentenced to 20 years in prison. I'm not sure what all happened in that 20 years he was incarcerated as a young Black boy with grown men, but I imagine it was someplace he never wanted to return. He had only been out three years before the fateful night, and as a grieving mother, I am left with so many unanswered questions. What actually happened? They said he had a gun on him, but no gun was ever found. They said he had a pill bottle with a white substance, but that was never found. Is the story made up? There is a long history of police lying to cover themselves (Ahmad Auberry, Breonna Taylor, Sandra Bland). How was being pulled over for a broken taillight worth engaging in a chase? Did they run him off the road on purpose? What was going through his mind in those final hours? What happened to him is still under investigation.

Abdul was only 13 when he moved to Hazelhurst, Georgia, and two years later he was arrested at 15 and served 20 years for robbery and kidnapping. They tried my son as an adult for these crimes when he was just a kid. He was released May 4th, 2017 at 35 and died on February 11th, 2020 at just 38 years old. Abdul was born September 19th, 1981, and I always called him my love child. It's ironic because he died in the love month, and we celebrated his life that month!

I was not there for my son, and now that I have it together, I decided to use my voice and my body (everything I have) to speak for other young men like him.

◆ ◆ ◆

I was at the La Mesa demonstration for only seven minutes before I was shot in the face with a "bean bag" that landed me in an ICU and with an eye that I can no longer use. The officer who shot me wanted to silence me, because my voice was the only weapon I had. My son came to me during the Life Flight, and he told me, "We ain't ready for you over here yet; you still have more struggles to go through." The night he passed, he came to me again while I was taking my bath and told me, "Don't be sad for me. I'm sad for what you have to go through."

In 2008 I entered Drug Core, and this program changed the direction of my life. It was an extensive, no bullshit program with a lot of structure—mostly, with me managing a sober living transitional house where I began working with a longtime friend I'd met years ago in a previous rehabilitation program. She had remained clean throughout her journey, and working with her helped give me build the foundation of continuous sobriety.

My son and I were both victims of what I call a "modern-day lynching without a tree." He's not here to tell his story, so I speak for him—today. And on that night when Officer Eric Knudsen shot me in my face with what they call a "projectile," or "bean bag," that nearly killed me, I was there for Abdul Jabar Rajai Furcron, my son.

I have lost the vision in my left eye. I've had one major surgery with the possibility of others in the future. I struggle now with driving. As I said, I'm a social butterfly, and I can't go as freely as I would like to anymore, especially with driving at night. My two sons—who are living—and my grandchildren are usually here to help me, and I'm appreciative of them, but I have lost my sense of security and independence. I now have glasses that I wear all day every day, regular doctor appointments, and my face that has been changed by this incident.

Looking at my face—one eyebrow is higher than the other, and a scar runs across the middle of my forehead—and the loss of vision in my left eye makes me angry. People tell me I look so good, but when I see my face, it's hard to accept.

Then God reaches and taps me and says: "You are living!" I still have purpose and reason to live! My son is there as part of my purpose because he came to me and said, "Not yet!" I'm thankful that Abdul saw me good, and was able to see my new lifestyle as a voice for him, because silence is violence, and I still got work to do! I also hope that one day I will regain vision in my left eye because my life has totally been changed from this. I want people to know that this was not called for, and I wish there could have been a different outcome.

Ebony is a parent currently grappling with living through a pandemic with two small children who are trying their best to do the same. She teaches English at San Diego City College and hopes her life as professor and parent is remembered as one led by love.

Ebony Tyree
From a Gap to a Gaping Hole

There was an engineer in the dock "when the levees broke" who explained the loud noise the residents heard from the Lower Ninth Ward in New Orleans "as the noise of a levee that broke from a gap to a gaping hole."

Some described it as a loud BOOM! And what proceeded was a massive flood.

I suppose this imagery describes my life right now. Living through a pandemic with two small children has destabilized every "levee" in my life that has held up throughout the years. I thought I was doing a pretty good job as a parent. I never received an unusual number of complaints about my kids from teachers. Occasionally, my son would have a bad day or my daughter would have an odd obsession with going to the nurse's office, but they were never in the principal's office or suspended or anything, so I figured I must be doing an okay job, right? Well, after spending this time at home with my children, I began recognizing a few gaps in my parenting.

When the country shut down due to the spread of COVID-19, we all began working from home. My children had been released from attending school; their teachers weren't prepared for the pandemic, and they really had no plan. Essentially, this made it a free-for-all for the kids. Meanwhile, I was still working from home, and it was within the first 30 days that I recognized a few parenting gaps.

One thing's for sure, I didn't realize my children ate so much and so frequently! Who knew? I would send them to school with a sack lunch. Most times they had something to eat for breakfast, but sometimes they wouldn't wake up early enough, and they might only get a piece of fruit. Then they'd come home and have dinner. I was under the assumption that this same food regimen would apply at home. However, it didn't! I missed the memo that when kids are home all day, they eat all day too! I suppose I had never spent so many days with my children in the home at once. What kind of parent doesn't know this?

Anyhow, their tendency to eat all day caused a lot of problems for all of us throughout the day. I'd be in class (via Zoom) or in a meeting, and one of my children (mainly my 5-year-old son) would come ask if he could make eggs and bacon. This would be in the middle of class. As recently as last week, my students continue to tease me about the request. The chat popped up from a student, "Hey, Professor, did your son make bacon today?"

These are the moments that would have never happened in a class before. My students would never know what was happening in my home or even know my kids so intimately. I don't know how I feel about this, but I appreciate the grace they have shown me in such times, and I continue to do the same for them. This shit is hard!

Then there was that time I was on a Zoom meeting, and my son wanted a hard-boiled egg. I'd like to start by saying I always prided myself in being an attentive parent, making sure my kids had food to eat, clean clothes, underwear, etcetera. I actually often buy extra toilet paper because I never want my kids to go without (all of which was a bit ironic when the pandemic hit, and folks were stocking up on toilet paper...I already had plenty). Anyhow, apparently, I hadn't fed my child, and he was so hungry that he attempted to boil an egg on his own—without water. When I realized what was happening, there was a half-burned egg—shell and all—in a pot with a huge crack. Nevertheless, the folks I was on Zoom with witnessed this all unfold, and we chuckled about it. Truth be told, we are all *still* telling the story and getting a chuckle out of it.

Seems like I laugh at myself more often these days, but I'm not sure if it's because this stuff is really funny, or that if I stopped laughing I'd start crying, so the humor I've developed in such a time has saved me. Of course, my son didn't find it amusing that we were laughing at his misfortune because he was actually hungry and, from his perspective, we were laughing at his failed attempt at making a hard-boiled egg. The reality is, we are all laughing as a "fix." This gaping hole needs to be filled with something...why not laughter?

Ahmad is a third-year student at the University of California, Berkeley. He's a student advocate and community organizer. Currently, he's one of two undergraduate student representatives on the Berkeley campus Independent Advisory Board on Police Accountability.

Ahmad Mahmoud

Why Do We Rebel?

The year was 2020.

I was screaming in pain, my eyes were burning as if acid had been tossed on my face, my throat was full of tear-gas, and I was struggling to breathe. I had been shot by the police! My first thought was to alert my family and friends. I struggled to write a Facebook post and, thankfully, I was eventually able to get a post up notifying the community of what happened on the scene.

What exactly led up to the moment? I don't know, but one thing was for sure: I can still vividly remember an almost-empty water bottle thrown from a distance connecting with the thick metal helmet worn by a La Mesa Police Department officer. Seconds later, dozens of peaceful demonstrators were shot and thousands more tear-gassed. I heard my name in the background, "Ahmad.... Ahmad.... AHMAAD!" I was clueless as to which direction my name was being called from. I tried looking around, but all I saw was smoke and people running. I did not recognize the San Diego I knew and loved. When I was able to get up and run toward Vons, fortunately, along the way, I ran into many of my friends and community members. They yelled my name.

"Ahmad.... Ahmad.... Oh, my God! Ahmad, are you okay?" I stared at them with little breath left in my lungs, burning eyes, and painful kidneys from being shot by a rubber bullet. I told them I was just fine.

They informed me that my cousin, Ismahan, had heard I was hurt and was looking for me, so I immediately went searching for her. I knew she would be worried, and I knew she would do anything to save my life, but I wanted her to know I was fine. When I finally found her, she hugged me and told me to not leave her side for the duration of the protest. She walked me to the Arco gas station across the street from the battleground, where an entire community was waiting for me. Each of them hugged me like the mother of a missing child who had just been found. I felt warm and tender with an entire community made up of people from all identities standing by my side. Later that night, when I charged my phone and it turned back on, I hopped on to Facebook and saw that I had over twenty-five notifications. I was shocked. What had happened? Did someone else get hurt? Did a loved one die? Did someone get arrested? No, no, and no. It was Laila Aziz, my big sister and shero, who made a Facebook post to have a search party find me after I had posted that I had gotten shot. More than two dozen people had commented, and even more had left their jobs and homes to find me. I felt love. I felt reassurance. I felt in community.

One might ask, why did I rebel that day? Why did I go to every demonstration from that day forward for two weeks straight? Well, this is why we rebel.

I had woken up that morning angry, angrier than I have ever been. I wasn't sure what to expect, but I was willing to put my life on the line for justice. Following the lead of cities all across the nation, especially Minneapolis, I knew this was the moment. A moment different from all other time periods I've lived through. For if justice was to prevail, this was the time to demand it. So, I took to the streets to participate in the rebellions. Having not yet confronted my feelings about the deaths of George Floyd, Breonna Taylor, and Ahmaud Arbery, anxiety, confusion, and hopelessness ran through my veins. However, like so many young people in the world, I recognized my responsibility to fight for justice.

To rebel, for me, is personal, and it begins with my mom.

The year was 1991.

*Civil war breaks out in Somalia. Civil war kills, and one woman,
Rahmo Bihi, sits, thinking about her impending death. Then she thinks
about her children. She determines that life is worth living and decides to
head for a refugee camp in Kenya. For five years, Rahmo struggles to maintain her sanity and support her children. She suffers through five years of
unimaginable unknowns. And, despite not knowing English or Western
culture, she decides to apply for refugee status in the US. Fortunately, her
application is accepted.*

Rahmo is my mother. Since 1996, she has been forced to work multiple minimum-wage jobs to provide for seven children. And still our
life has been hard—for her, for me, and for my six siblings. I remember
nights when my mother would not be able to feed us. She would tell us
to sleep and I did, hoping that there would be breakfast in the morning,
only to awake to more nothing. I remember treading to school with a
rumbling belly. All the other children smiled, and their parents would
hug them while dropping them off. But my mother could not hug me
at the school gate because she would be at her job. For much of my life,
I faced the struggle and blessing of living nearly on my own, with some
exceptions.

My mother did not speak English, and no one went out of their way
to communicate in Somali. I was the liaison between my family and all of
America. I went everywhere with my mother as her personal translator.

Then there was high school. For many, it is an obligation, determined
by their parents or the government, but my version of high school was
different; high school was my home. It was my only safe space. It was
where I was exposed to the concepts of race, gender, colonialism and
more. My friends and I shared books on capitalism, incarceration, and
history. My friend group was made up of Black, Latinx, Asian, and Indigenous students. My experiences from existing in this shared space of education would forever change my outlook on life. At the same time, it
was the first time I had a fuller understanding of my identity as a young

Black, Somali Muslim. However, while school served as a distraction, my home life was a complete wreck.

When I was 13 years old, during my freshman year, my oldest brother began abusing drugs and other intoxicants. Night after night, he would come home unstable. He argued incessantly with my mother. And soon he drew blood. First from my mom, then from me. I felt hopeless and many nights I'd cry myself to sleep. My brother had single-handedly taken away my safe space. Most of my freshman peers in high school were worried about clubs, sports, and friends; all I ever worried about was peace and safety. This is often the reality of many low-income, BIPOC youth.

My mother and I were trapped in another civil war. As a freshman I began to stay home from school to prevent my brother from wreaking more havoc. I attended court hearings, doctors' appointments, and any other interaction my mother had with the outside world. She had sacrificed her life to escape the civil war in Somalia for me, and I was willing to sacrifice my education to mitigate the civil war in our home. My home life was taking a toll on my academics, and my grades for my first year of high school would serve as evidence.

On the first day of my sophomore year, my mother told me in Somali, "Ahmad, just focus on your school; the rest is up to me." I had struggled and grown without encouragement, but her words, mixed with her struggle, motivated me. I decided to move forward. My mother had always had the opportunity to give up, whether it was during her fight for survival to find refuge in America or her determination not to call the police to incriminate my brother. Never a fan of law enforcement, to this day she vividly remembers when SDPD shot and killed her cousin who battled schizophrenia. She had a strong sense of faith and never surrendered. She always saw the best in people and, in her own way, practiced restorative justice. My mother might have grown up in a country where everyone was the same race, but she understood clearly that her children were different here in the United States. We had more melanin in our skin, which would change the trajectory of our lives in this racist country. So, she was very careful and cautious when it comes to us.

After that conversation with my mother during my sophomore year, every time I think about quitting, I remember her words, and then I remember her sacrifice. Her struggles defined the future man I seek to be. In 1991, she put escape at the top of her priorities. In 2015, as a high school sophomore, I put fighting for justice at the top of mine.

So, why do we rebel? It is because we have no other choice. Today, I organize around racial justice, researching alternative models for public safety and supporting both incarcerated and formerly incarcerated peoples. I want a world where everyone has a home, access to healthcare, education, a livable wage, and a police-, prison-, and war-free society.

Julieta Barajas was born in Guadalajara, Jalisco, Mexico. Currently, she is 18 years old and is a first-generation college student at San Diego City College. She believes that she is who she is today because of everything that has happened in her life, and is proud to say that she will keep fighting for a better future for coming generations.

Julieta P. Barajas

Aprendí a Vivir, I Learned to Live

When I was about four years old, I moved from Guadalajara to the US when my mom married my stepdad, Julio. At first, everything was fine. It was as if he was trying to win her over by giving me gifts. I didn't mind at the time. I mean, what five-year-old wouldn't like toys, right? But as I grew older, my parents had two more kids, and as they came along, I stopped receiving the attention I wanted. I guess I felt different, especially because I knew he was not my biological dad, so I saw the way he treated his kids, and it was much different than how he treated me. I suddenly became the responsible older sister that had to babysit, clean, remain quiet, and not talk back. And I was scared for a long time; I was scared of my dad; I was scared that I would disappoint him, since he always told me I had everything because of him and him only, so I felt like I owed him everything.

When I started to enter my teenage years, something changed inside of him, and he began to constantly fight with my mom. I called the cops on him at least five times throughout my childhood. The fights were stupid, but soon after, the little fights became big fights, and as much as I was afraid of who he became, my siblings and mom were my priority; I felt a need to protect them. My dad noticed I took my mom's side a lot, and this angered him and made him attack me over little situations.

His childhood was rough, and he always talked about it with my mom. I overheard these stories and felt sad that he was kicked out at 16 and had to live on his own. I thought to myself, Wow, his mom was horrible. Hearing stories about how he had never had any of the things I had

97

had as a child made me feel bad for him, but my attempts to make excuses for him came to an end when I caught him cheating on my mom. That experience crushed me. I went to a Guns N' Roses concert with him in 2017 and felt so happy that for once we would have some father-daughter bonding, something I had craved for so long. But at one point that night, I caught him texting this woman named Stephanie, saying he missed her. At that moment my stomach sank. I thought about my mom and how she would be heartbroken. I ended up telling her, and she cried, and nothing makes me angrier than a person who makes my mom cry. From then on, I distanced myself from him. No talking, just tension.

With quarantine starting back in March of 2020, I read that the number of cases of domestic violence had spiked up tremendously, with one of those cases being my family. As my siblings, mom, stepdad, and I stayed at home for several weeks, he became more aggressive every day. He tried to make it up to us by buying us stuff, but I didn't care for his stupid ways—he couldn't buy his forgiveness. Every day was a struggle to balance family, job, and school. I picked up after him when he finished eating, I cleaned the house, took care of my dog, and I still spent time with him, not to mention the amount of homework I had piling up. My mental health was going down the drain. I was so unhappy I spent my nights crying.

Well, as you would expect, everyone has a limit and my limit was on June 7, 2020. My stepdad had been babbling to my mom, calling her names, insulting her family, and on top of that, insulting me. I knew I was about to explode, so I got up from the table to go shower, until he demanded I sit down. I told him no, that I needed to go to the restroom, but he said he didn't care. I was so angry I told him no at the same time my mom was yelling at me to listen to him. I told her: "No, it's not fair. He thinks he can control whoever he wants." At that moment he got up and hit me. My mom yelled at him to stop, but I was full of adrenaline, so I went at him, and pushed him back. My mom got in between us, begging us to stop while he kept trying to hit me. My sister came out of her room to see what was going on, but he grabbed her and pushed her. I was enraged; he had no reason to start fighting with her.

I was crying from anger, yelling at my mom and saying how could she stay with such a person who doesn't even have respect for his daughters. I ended up calling the cops because he had elbowed my little sister's neck, ripped my mom's skin, and cut my leg. They took him away, and I filed for a restraining order. He made bail but only had enough money to cover him for a couple of months. He kept begging my mom and me for forgiveness, but I turned cold. I was no longer the same person I had been. I was no longer the little girl who depended on him for everything.

So, I ignored him and didn't even acknowledge his presence when he came to see his kids. I wouldn't talk to him or say hello. My mom, on the other hand, still had a soft spot for him. She felt bad that he was living in hotels and buying out to eat, but then again, I knew it was just his way of manipulating her. If there's one good thing about me, it's that I can tell whenever someone is lying or trying to manipulate, because I lived with it for 15 years.

Long story short, she let him back in the house, and I was really mad.

My mom promised me that this time would be different and that I wouldn't even need to talk to him. And for a short time, it was. Eventually, however, he demanded the respect that I had already lost. I decided I would no longer keep my feelings bottled up just because he wanted to feel "respected." A fight occurred one day during dinner when I had brought my partner home, since Julio had invited us over for a meal. Everything was fine until I got on my phone to check if a biology assignment I had was due that night or if it was marked late. This angered my stepdad, I suppose, and he said out loud: "Hah, even the girls who are supposed to be an example fail to do so."

My partner, Isabel, who was also checking her assignments, felt uncomfortable, so she put the phone down. But me? Nope.

He said, "Did you not hear me?" as I scrolled on my Canvas page.

I responded, "I heard you."

Then he said, "See, Patti, she never listens!" My mom asked me to put my phone down, so I did. That's when the arguments between me and him began.

He said, "Why are you still living here? I don't want you here. No one wants you here. You cause problems between everyone." I thought that was pretty funny because everyone in my family loves me, especially since I helped them and was there for them whenever he went into his psycho mode.

"Say whatever you think will help your ego, Julio," I replied. He got even more mad at this and started insulting me. Whatever, I was used to it. After dinner, I went to finish a lab I had for biology. It was then that he started saying that he was kicking me out and to pack my stuff and leave. Trust me when I say I was way ahead of him, but my mom stopped me. She said I wasn't doing things right, and I said I wasn't going to stand him much longer. The night ended with him trying to apologize since I called the cops. But they didn't take him away because he hadn't hit any of us during that particular incident.

I moved out of the house about three days later; it was sad leaving my mom and siblings, but I was tired and done. I'm fine with him affecting my emotional side, but when it comes to school and the fact that he made me miss a section test in biology that was worth 50 points, that's where I am not okay. It's been two weeks since I moved out, and I'm happy to say my mental health has never been better. I am free now, and I can focus on my school and myself during this pandemic.

In the end, my stepdad changed me in all ways possible: He made me weak and strong, he taught me good and bad, he brought me love and hate. I would say he changed me in the way of defending myself and not taking any bullshit from anyone. But I had to learn to become the person I am now by facing him. I sometimes wish that things could have ended differently between us, but I know now that I will never get along with him because he doesn't respect women, and most importantly, he doesn't respect his own daughters or wife. There are many emotionally traumatic moments that still replay in my head, and sometimes when I lie in bed at night, my heart starts pounding, and I cry out of fear of him hurting me. I guess I still am weak, or maybe I'm just human. I will learn to overcome it. After all, today I am living on my own, going to school, working and trying to hold everything together.

Laila has spent the majority of her life in Southeast San Diego. Her most memorable experiences occurred before a backdrop of palm trees, low riders, taco shops, and canyons. She is a Seventies baby, who came into existence dancing to the wail of electric guitars. Her DNA is a hybrid of soul and funk. She is the child of protestors, resisters, and revolutionaries. She is one generation after Jim Crow, conceived in the midst of redlining. She came of age in the prison industrial complex boom, where living in a cage became America's latest rage.

Laila Aziz

The Fire This Time

I did not plan on going to the La Mesa protest, in a San Diego suburb that on most occasions was a slow, unassuming town. I had already had a long dialogue with my inner activist concerning the little change we had seen with the initial demonstration. Even after long marches and a hoarse voice, the police continued to murder us with impunity. Even after proof of systemic racism in the courts, the San Diego District Attorneys continued to evolve into a series of defense experts when law enforcement was concerned. The legislature always watered down our most robust bills after heavy police union lobbying. Billy Venable was murdered in my community in 2003, unarmed. The District Attorney said the shooting was justified, claiming Venable was reaching for the officer's gun. Forensics ruled that he never could have had his hands on the officer's gun, because the officer was lying on his weapon the entire time. As for La Mesa, we were also in the middle of a pandemic, and I could not rationalize bringing a potential death sentence to my family after a pointless protest. But then....

I watched the Facebook Lives and sat mortified. My chest tightened and my hands began to shake uncontrollably as I witnessed the police throw tear-gas and shoot rubber bullets at peaceful protestors. I watched the protestors' anger and pain erupt as the La Mesa Police Department and the San Diego Sheriff treated the mostly young crowd like animals. They circled them like prey, brutalizing them with rubber bullets. We have long ceased to fight a battle based on civil rights, but as Malcolm X eloquently stated in a 1964 letter to the *Egyptian Gazette*: "The common goal of 22 million Afro-Americans is respect as human beings, the God given right to be a human being. Our common goal is to obtain the human rights America has been denying us. We can never get civil rights in America until our human rights are first restored. We will never be recognized as citizens there until we are first recognized as humans."

Affected by what I heard and saw online, I secured a last-minute babysitter and drove to La Mesa. The scene was utter chaos. The police presence was heavy, and smoke engulfed the small San Diego suburb. To many, La Mesa symbolizes the American Dream: small, quaint homes, specialty shops, and ethnic restaurants nestled before a backdrop of Western glory. Western glory, which ignores the indigenous Kumeyaay, their land snatched as they succumbed to steel and disease, and violently converted to Catholicism. La Mesa, engulfed in flames, was now the epicenter of a human rights struggle against state-sanctioned violence after witnesses captured a young Black man falsely accused of assaulting a white officer. On Saturday, May 30th, 2020, the sleepy community was no longer a symbol of a staid, compliant town. Every block screamed violence as officers patrolled sections with billy clubs in hand. La Mesa now was the scene of an elderly, Black grandmother who was shot in the head by a bean bag, shocking us all as we witnessed it lodged in her skull. Her sin, throwing an empty aluminum soda can in frustration. The protestors were now on fire. Anger rippled throughout the entire city.

Within five minutes of parking, I turned the corner on a quiet residential street, shocked as the Chase Bank became engulfed in flames. As I crossed the road and entered the trolley platform, I stood in the middle of La Mesa Boulevard, the right and left side of my face stinging from the heat as I marveled at how capitalism, racism, sexism, exploitation, oppression, and poverty symbolically burned to the ground when that institution fell beneath its own flames. Chase Bank and Union Bank of California were both on fire. Is this what James Baldwin meant when he detailed the civil rights struggle in his book *The Fire Next Time*?

I may be America's problem, as W.E.B. Du Bois firmly stated, but I am not America's only problem. Its children today are also fed up with its nonsense and demand a better world. Thousands upon thousands of white youth pillaged the streets. Many of them screaming, "Black Lives Matter." They wrote "Fuck 12" on wall after wall, solidifying their stance against the police state.

This country has never made amends for not only chattel slavery but Jim Crow, lynching, redlining, domestic terrorism, land theft, rape, and mass incarceration. It has reinvented oppression decade after decade, allowing "racially neutral" whites to walk their dogs, push their strollers on perfectly paved sidewalks, pass picket fences, and pretend Black and Brown people don't live under constant, daily occupation and state-sanctioned violence. They have recalibrated their propaganda to maintain racism, and instead of calling us niggers we are now criminals. This is the bullshit they rock themselves to sleep with every night, and when their fantasy explodes, their true colors come out, "Kill them all!" They have allowed capitalism and its foundation built on slavery to evolve into systems of local and global oppression, utilizing the police forces to remove anything suspicious from their community as they uphold human rights violations while singing hymns in church.

I have been followed out of all-white neighborhoods by police cars, which seem to follow me until I reach an area where I belong. I have been brutalized by police officers in San Diego's suburbs, my face plowed into the concrete with rifles pointed at my head. My crime, being in an area I did not belong. I have been corralled like cattle back into my own neighborhood by San Diego's gang unit, whose sole purpose is to violate the rights of Black and Brown people.

America's demise will not come from outside forces—America will implode. It will collapse from the inside, its rotten, stinking guts spilling into both seas. The suburbs will become the focal point of the struggle, as Black and Brown people are murdered by police after crossing their invisible lines. Their economic borders will be their demise as people rise up throughout the nation, bringing human rights demands to their immaculate lawns. Parents, who have become so occupied with pretending their family structure remains intact and healthy, have offered their children a future full of toxins. Westernization has reached its plateau. American exceptionalism offers the world nothing of significance, because it would rather destroy the entire planet than concede it must change direction or destroy everything within its reach. They have chosen to murder us all, even themselves, in an effort to preserve the power of accumulation, global exploitation, and in its most abhorrent pathological state, its ability to destroy anything that challenges its position in the world.

I hear the suburban outrage: How dare they burn the banks! How dare they riot and loot. Not once do they try to comprehend Black rage, a demand to be acknowledged as human. The demand that police officers lying on Black men and destroying their lives in the criminal justice system is more important than any piece of concrete building. Sitting in cages, like animals, for being Black and Brown, is the injustice. Anything else is the product of injustice. Their children have begun to understand. They have demanded economic systems that don't spit toxins into the air. They have insisted on the elimination of plastic pollutants piling on the earth. They have envisioned a world where caste systems, racism, patriarchy, parasitic capitalism, rape, oppression, and all other isms and schisms based on harm are eliminated.

The fire this time will burn, as La Mesa proved, on America's main streets.

afterword

2020 Is the Culmination of a Generation of Disregard Toward the Poor and Most Vulnerable Among Us

Darius Spearman

How 2020 will be remembered depends on the backdrop that set the stage for a dramatic and tumultuous year. The year began as a mysterious pathogen that few had heard of in January 2020 ultimately transformed millions of lives within the span of just a few months. By mid-March of 2020, students' lives were thrown into chaos as schools and universities were forced to switch to fully online instruction mid-semester in the face of the COVID-19 pandemic. Simultaneously, social justice activism was tested not only by the deadly virus but by ongoing state repression. This all occurred on top of a health care system that had already been failing many but especially Black, Brown, and poor communities. The two combined to make mass protest more dangerous than any time since civil rights activists faced down fire hoses and police dogs. The abrupt shift compounded the already ongoing battles for basic dignity, health, and the right to simply exist without fear of police violence. Those struggles now had to continue in the era of social distancing, live streaming, and overt encouragement of police violence from the Office of the President.

The current state of affairs sits atop a foundation of disregard for the poorest and most vulnerable of society. Denial of science, denial of police violence, and the denial of humanity of immigrant populations stems not from a lack of belief but rather from a lack of regard. Not from disbelief but rather the belief that because these issues primarily impact Black, Brown, and poor communities, they are not worthy of our collective concern.

As people fought for their lives on the streets of La Mesa, they braved police repression and a deadly global pandemic. As difficult as it was to observe social distancing while engaged in mass protest, they took precautions as best they could and masked up. Meanwhile, those who denied the severity of the pandemic dismissed the CDC guidelines and went maskless—once again secure in their belief that the pandemic would only affect "certain people" as it ripped through prisons and immigrant detention centers. After receiving the best treatment taxpayers' money could buy to treat his COVID, President Donald Trump proceeded to re-enter the White House maskless (Poo). In doing so, he endangered the folks who attended to him and demonstrated his general disregard of the Black and Latinx populations who have borne the brunt of the COVID-19 crisis. Countless "Kens" and "Karens" throughout the country ignored or openly defied mask mandates based on recommendations from the Centers for Disease Control (CDC). Rather than follow the public health directions for slowing the spread of the disease, they insisted that wearing a mask constituted an assault on their freedom.

Meanwhile, CDC data "suggests a disproportionate burden of illness and death among racial and ethnic minority groups.... [E]very time there is a major public health concern...[t]he most vulnerable and underresourced are the most severely affected." In addition, Black and Latinx people "make up a large percentage of essential workers, such as grocery clerks, transit workers, and hospital staff, among others, putting them at greater risk of exposure [to COVID-19]" (Johnson).

As of January 15, 2021, over 50,000 Black and over 60,000 Latinx lives were lost to COVID-19 (APM). Black and Latinx people are *nearly three times more likely to die from COVID-19 infection than whites* ("Risk"). We did not see videos of their deaths go viral on social media. They did not have the knee of a policeman deliberately murdering them. But too many died because of the passive and active disregard for their lives and their humanity. Like George Floyd, they could not breathe.

The narratives within this volume attest to a generation of disregard leading up to 2020 that effectively sandwiched Black and Brown communities between the invisible peril of COVID-19 and the visible peril of police aggression.

A comprehensive history of police violence would begin with the slave patrols at the beginning of the 1700s. A framework for current policing, however, might begin with the civil rights protests in the 1950s and 60s. Through the centuries, as Black people used the legal system to combat oppression, many police aligned with white mobs, using terror tactics to thwart Black protest while also arresting them for civil disobedience (Agyepong 255).

The movement against police violence that we see in many of the narratives in this text has its roots in the 2013 fatal shooting of 14-year-old Trayvon Martin by vigilante George Zimmerman. Zimmerman's subsequent acquittal gave rise to protests across the United States, where the Black Lives Matter hashtag was created to address anti-blackness in communities across the country.

"Black Lives Matter" became the slogan used to mobilize against the deaths of Black people as a result of police and vigilante violence. Consistent with the historical pattern of police backlash against Black resistance movements, "Blue Lives Matter" became yet another Twitter hashtag on December 20, 2014. Soon thereafter, "All Lives Matter" was added to the slogans. In this way, the doctrine of colorblindness actively promoted continued violence on Black and Brown people. Findings show that there was not "evidence of a significant discussion of 'all lives'" (Gallagher 18). In fact, the hashtag was actually utilized to discuss police lives and to assert that Black people were hazards to the lives of law enforcement officers and their efforts to protect "Americans."

The counterattack on those criticizing police violence by painting protestors as violent was later fueled by President Trump when he referred to the football players who knelt in solidarity with Black Lives Matter during the national anthem as "sons of bitches" (Kurtz). In 2020, the police murder of George Floyd became the flashpoint that culminated a generation of disregard for police violence against Black and Brown people while laying the backdrop for many of the narratives contained in this volume.

As will become significant in the case of Amaurie Johnson (discussed below), the issues Black and Brown communities face usually do not make headlines. Such issues include the practice of "carding." In both the United States and Canada, "police will stop a civilian on the street, usually also sometimes in their cars, and the fundamental reason they are stopped is unapparent. When you're stopped, you are asked to provide police with identification which they record and store in a police database" (Clarke). Because a record of numerous interactions with police can be used against them in criminal cases, the practice of "carding" effectively criminalizes the Black, Brown, and poor communities subjected to it. Pillars of the Community has made a focus of the most glaring outcome of these practices—gang documentation and enhancement. (Harvey and Duncan). In fact, Black people are three times more likely to get carded, leading to increased incarceration rates among Black and Brown people (Clarke).

On May 27, 2020, Amaurie Johnson was waiting for a friend near a luxury apartment complex in La Mesa when two officers manhandled and arrested him. According to Johnson's subsequent lawsuit, "Officer Dages refused to believe that the black man in athletic gear would have friends that live in a luxury apartment complex. Officer Dages challenged Mr. Johnson to call his friends to prove his reason for being there.

The conduct was done on reasons rooted in the fact that Mr. Johnson is black" (Gregorio-Nieto). In response to the police abuse against Johnson, and in the wake of the police murder of Gorge Floyd, a Chase Bank was destroyed in La Mesa during the ensuing unrest on May 30, 2020.

In typical fashion, the press heavily emphasized the "violence" against buildings and property while all but ignoring police violence against Black and Brown bodies. One article in particular made no mention of injuries inflicted on any persons. Nor did it make any mention of the violence inflicted on Amaurie Johnson. It did, however, equate the damage to two local banks with violence. "Chase Bank...was torched during Saturday's violent demonstrations.... Two ATMs at the [Union Bank] branch sustained fire damage but were not otherwise vandalized" (Freeman). As the reader will note, there were at least two protesters in these narratives alone who were injured by police projectiles during the protests in La Mesa, but there was no mention in this article of the police violence that resulted in their *bodily* injury (see Ahmad Mahmuod, "Why Do We Rebel?" and Leslie Furcron, "Abdul Jabar Rajai Furcron, or Leslie's Story"). The disregard for Black and Brown lives in favor of property had also been building in immigrant communities over the past generation.

Hostility towards immigration waxes and wanes with the economic cycles in this country. There are calls for relaxing restrictions when favorable economic conditions require an increase in workers and calls for tighter restrictions during economic downturns. California's Proposition 187 marked a turning point in the rhetoric. In 1994, Republican Assemblyman Dick Mountjoy introduced a California ballot initiative that required law enforcement to investigate the immigration status of any detainees they might suspect of being unlawful immigrants. Billed as the "Save our State" initiative, California's Proposition 187 further required government agents, as well as school and healthcare employees, to deny publicly-funded services to persons they suspected of being undocumented and in some cases to report those persons to immigration authorities.

Even while later court challenges found the measure unconstitutional, with its passage by 59% of California voters, the ballot initiative did significantly ratchet up anti-immigrant rhetoric. Suddenly, it wasn't enough to simply say that immigrants were sucking up public resources. Glen Spencer, an anti-immigrant activist who organized border patrols of the US–Mexican border, argued that Proposition 187 was necessary because illegal immigration was part of a reconquest of the American Southwest. He posed the inflammatory question, "Do we want to retain control of the Southwest more than the Mexicans want take it from us?" (Adams 36):

> It was a territorial-based, particularly anti-Mexican rhetoric. Let me quote you some examples from a couple of the leaders of various organizations promoting 187. Betty Hammond, who you still see in the newspapers, said this about Mexican immigrants: "They come here, they have their babies, and after they become citizens, and all those children use social services." The threat is that somehow Mexicans are going to reproduce and take over the Southwest. (Adams 35-36)

After September 11, 2001, both the anti-immigrant fervor and the state repression of dissent gained even further momentum. Following the al-Qaeda attacks on the World Trade Center and the Pentagon, the "Federal Bureau of Investigation (FBI) and the Immigration and Naturalization Service took some 1,200 (largely Muslim and/or Arab) noncitizens residing in the United States into custody, many without charge, amid rampant reports of abuse" (Vasi 1717).

Both the House and the Senate, Democrats and Republicans, formulated a hasty response in the form of the Uniting and Strengthening America by Providing Appropriate Tools Required to Intercept and Obstruct Terrorism Act (more popularly known as "The USA PATRIOT

Act"). Submitted to the Congress on October 23, 2001, the 342-page bill passed the House a day later by a vote of 357 to 66, "grant[ing] federal agencies broad powers to conduct searches, use electronic surveillance, and detain suspected terrorists" (Vasi 1719). The following day, the Senate passed the Patriot Act by a vote of 98 to 1, and the very next day, the Patriot Act was signed into law by President George W. Bush.

The impact on Black and Brown communities came swiftly. Only days after the attacks on September 11, the former Reform Party presidential candidate, Patrick Buchanan, "proposed a moratorium on immigration, rapid expansion of the US Border Patrol, and the deportation of 'eight-to-eleven million illegal aliens, beginning with those from rogue nations'" (qtd. in Vasi 1734). In addition, "The Justice Department's inspector general reported that 7,000 people have complained of abuse and countless others don't even know that they've been subjected to a search because the law requires that they be kept secret" (Vasi 1720).

Predictably, public sentiment showed little sympathy with regard to the attack on civil liberties so long as that attack was primarily directed toward Black and Brown people. "According to a Pew Center study, in the weeks following 9/11 a majority of Americans believed it would be necessary to sacrifice some personal freedoms to fight terrorism effectively" (Vasi 1728). The public willingness to sacrifice freedom for security was the final piece in the culmination of events that led to a presidency that brought out the worst tendencies among us.

Donald J. Trump made clear his intention to capitalize on those tendencies in his June 16, 2015 speech announcing his candidacy for president. More alarming than his often bizarre campaign promises was the adulation with which they were met. In his speech, he promised to stop implementation of the Affordable Care Act, he promised to build a wall along the US/Mexico border and make Mexico pay for it, and most infamously said of Mexican immigrants, "When Mexico sends its people, they're not sending their best.... They're sending people that have lots of problems and they're bringing those problems with us [sic]. They're bringing drugs, they're bringing crime, they're bringing rapists, and some, I assume, are good people" (qtd. in Elving).

Trump's anti-immigrant, anti-Muslim, anti-dissent, and anti-Black-and-Brown rhetoric would become the cornerstone of his candidacy, and later his presidency. Trump made clear his disdain for dissent and protest. Protesters at his rallies were met with open calls for hostility. When a protester was escorted out of his February 22, 2016 rally, he told a cheering crowd, "I'd like to punch him in the face, I tell ya." He continued, "I love the old days. You know what they used to do to guys like that when they were in a place like this? They'd be carried out on a stretcher, folks" (Miller). Later, during his presidency, he told a crowd of police officers in a July 27, 2017 speech:

> Now, we're getting them [criminals] out anyway, but we'd like to get them out a lot faster, and when you see these towns and when you see these thugs being thrown into the back of a paddy wagon, you just see them thrown in, rough, I said, please don't be too nice. Like when you guys put somebody in the car and you're protecting their head, you know, the way you put their hand over, like, don't hit their head and they've just killed somebody. Don't hit their head. I said, you can take the hand away, okay? (Miller)

As president, Trump's "zero tolerance" policy toward immigration also fed off the anti-immigrant sentiment that had been building over the past generation. The policy of mass detention of those seeking asylum paid no regard to the 4,368 children separated from their parents or guardians by January of 2020 ("Family Separation"). Not only was there disregard for immigrant families, but in the midst of a global pandemic, anti-immigrant disregard collided with contempt for science. Anyone versed in the US Prison Industrial Complex would not be surprised by the jarring reports. From July 13 to October 3, 2020, a research team, consisting of Physicians for Human Rights and the Harvard Medical School, sought to document the experience of immigrant detainees by conducting interviews of immigrants formerly detained by Immigration and Customs Enforcement (ICE). Among their findings, "Nearly all immigrants interviewed were unable to maintain social distance throughout the detention center." Additionally, "Out of all respondents who reported symptoms, only 17 percent (three people) were appropriately isolated from the general population and tested for COVID-19, one of whom tested positive" (Peeler). Perhaps most alarmingly:

> Forty-three study participants (86 percent) stated that they reported and/or protested about issues related to COVID-19, including verbally complaining to staff about unsanitary conditions or lack of personal protective equipment, filing formal grievances, going on hunger strikes, reporting conditions to lawyers, reporting conditions to the media, and sending messages to family members with the hope they would be publicized. Of these 43 who protested, 56 percent (24 people) reported experiencing acts of intimidation and retaliation after their complaints, including verbal abuse by detention facility staff, being pepper sprayed, being placed in solitary confinement, and experiencing threats or actions of limiting food, communication, or commissary access. (Peeler)

For all the data and percentages I have cited above, there is a story. A small sample of that story can be found in the narratives of Briseida Salazar, "No Lo Firmen! Don't Sign It!" and Anne Marie Rios, "My Heart Has a River in It."

With this historical backdrop, I have strived to establish the setting for the narratives within this volume. These stories are set upon a generation of disregard culminating in a president who channeled the worst aspects of the past 30 years—lack of regard for the science of public health, lack of regard for the violence inflicted on Black and Brown people at the hands of the police and vigilantes, and lack of regard for immigrant communities. Regard for the safety of property over people, however, is alive and well. It was the worst tendencies of the past 30 years that made a Trump presidency possible. As of this writing, Trump is set to leave office within a week, but the stage remains set for someone else to tap into those same tendencies if we fail to take heed of the voices within this volume.

Works Cited

Adams, Ruth S., et al. "Immigration: Proposition 187, Five Years Later." *Bulletin of the American Academy of Arts and Sciences*, vol. 53, no. 5, 2000, pp. 28-50. *JSTOR*, www.jstor.org/stable/3824572. Accessed 10 Jan. 2021.

Agyepong, Tera. "In the Belly of the Beast: Black Policemen Combat Police Brutality in Chicago, 1968-1983." *The Journal of African American History*, vol. 98, no. 2, 2013, pp. 253-276. *JSTOR*, www.jstor.org/stable/10.5323/jafriamerhist.98.2.0253.

APM Research Lab Staff. "The Color of Coronavirus: COVID-19 Deaths by Race and Ethnicity." *APM Research Lab*, 5 March 2021, www.apmresearchlab.org/covid/deaths-by-race.

Clarke, Kinsey. "Here's What Black Lives Matter Looks Like in Canada." *NPR*, 7 Aug. 2015, www.npr.org/sections/codeswitch/2015/08/07/427729459/heres-what-black-lives-matter-looks-like-in-canada.

Elving, Ron. "With Latest Nativist Rhetoric, Trump Takes America Back to Where It Came From." *NPR*, 16 July 2019, www.npr.org/2019/07/16/742000247/with-latest-nativist-rhetoric-trump-takes-america-back-to-where-it-came-from.

"Family Separation Under the Trump Administration—A Timeline." *The Southern Poverty Law Center*, 17 June 2020, www.splcenter.org/news/2020/06/17/family-separation-under-trump-administration-timeline.

Freeman, Mike. "Chase and Union Bank Look to Adapt After La Mesa Branches Torched During Protests." *The San Diego Union-Tribune*, 1 June 2020, www.sandiegouniontribune.com/business/story/2020-06-01/chase-and-union-bank-look-to-adapt-after-la-mesa-branches-torched-during-protests.

Gallagher, Ryan J., et al. "Divergent Discourse Between Protests and Counter-Protests: #BlackLivesMatter and #AllLivesMatter." *PLoS ONE*, vol. 13, no. 4, 2018. https://doi.org/10.1371/journal.pone.0195644.

Gregorio-Nieto, Brenda et al. "Amaurie Johnson Files Suit Against City of La Mesa, LMPD Officer." *NBC 7 San Diego*, 30 July 2020, www.nbcsandiego.com/news/local/amaurie-johnson-files-suit-against-city-of-la-mesa-lmpd/2374993/.

Harvey, Aaron, and Brandon "Tiny Doo" Duncan, guest lecuturers. "Guest Lecture: Guilty by Association? Aaron Harvey and Brandon 'Tiny Doo' Duncan Speak at San Diego City College," *African Elements*, 12 June 2015, africanelements.org/guest-lecture-guilty-by-association-aaron-harvey-and-brandon-tiny-doo-duncan-speak-at-san-diegocity-college/.

Johnson, Greg. "COVID-19's Assault on Black and Brown Communities." *Penn Today*, 26 May 2020, penntoday.upenn.edu/news/covid-19s-assault-black-and-brown-communities. Accessed 13 Jan. 2021.

Kurtz, Jason. "Trump 'SOB' Remark Moves NFL Player to Kneel During Anthem." *CNN*, 2017, www.cnn.com/2017/09/25/politics/dolphins-tight-end-julius-thomas-national-anthem-kneel-erin-burnett-outfront-cnntv/index.html.

Miller, Michael E. "Donald Trump on a Protester: 'I'd Like to Punch Him in the Face.'" *The Washington Post*, 23 Feb. 2016, www.washingtonpost.com/news/morning-mix/wp/2016/02/23/donald-trump-on-protester-id-like-to-punch-him-in-the-face/. Accessed 30 Apr. 2019.

Peeler, Katherine. "Praying for Hand Soap and Masks." *Physicians for Human Rights*, 12 Jan. 2021, phr.org/our-work/resources/praying-for-hand-soap-and-masks/. Accessed 16 Jan. 2021.

Poo, Ai-jen. "Trump Flouts COVID-19 Safety Rules with 'Utter Disregard' for White House Domestic Staff," *Democracy Now!*, 12 Oct. 2020, www.democracynow.org/2020/10/12/ai_jen_poo_trump_white_house.

"Risk for COVID-19 Infection, Hospitalization, and Death by Race/Ethnicity." *Centers for Disease Control and Prevention*, 16 July 2021, www.cdc.gov/coronavirus/2019-ncov/covid-data/investigations-discovery/hospitalization-death-by-race-ethnicity.html.

Vasi, Ion Bogdan, and David Strang. "Civil Liberty in America: The Diffusion of Municipal Bill of Rights Resolutions After the Passage of the USA PATRIOT Act." *American Journal of Sociology*, vol. 114, no. 6, 2009, pp. 1716-64. *JSTOR*, www.jstor.org/stable/10.1086/597177. Accessed 10 Jan. 2021.

Works Consulted

Casiano, Louis. "George Zimmerman Gets Probation in Stalking of Investigator Linked to Trayvon Martin Film Series." *Fox News*, 17 Nov. 2018, www.foxnews.com/us/george-zimmerman-receives-year-probation-in-stalking-case.

Chapple, Reshawna L., et al. "Do #BlackLivesMatter? Implicit Bias, Institutional Racism and Fear of the Black Body." *Ralph Bunche Journal of Public Affairs*, vol. 6, no. 1, article 2, 2017. *Digital Scholarship @ Texas Southern University*, digitalscholarship.tsu.edu/rbjpa/vol6/iss1/2.

Lavan, Makeba. "The Negro Tweets His Presence: Black Twitter As Social and Political Watchdog." *Modern Language Studies*, vol. 45, no. 1, 2015, pp. 56-65. *JSTOR*, www.jstor.org/stable/24616765.

Linscott, Charles "Chip" P. "Introduction: #BlackLivesMatter and the Mediatic Lives of a Movement." *Black Camera*, vol. 8, no. 2, 2017, pp. 75-80. *JSTOR*, www.jstor.org/stable/10.2979/blackcamera.8.2.04.

Mundt, Marcia, et al. "Scaling Social Movements Through Social Media: The Case of Black Lives Matter." *Social Media + Society*, Oct.-Dec. 2018, pp. 1-14. *Sage Journals*, doi.org/10.1177/2056305118807911.

Sue, Derald Wing. "The Invisible Whiteness of Being: Whiteness, White Supremacy, White Privilege, and Racism." *Addressing Racism: Facilitating Cultural Competence in Mental Health and Educational Settings*, edited by Madonna G. Constantine and Derald Wing Sue, Wiley, 2006, pp. 15-30.

Washington, Bryan. "Black Athletes Are Black People, and Black People Are Dying." *BuzzFeed News*, 25 Sept. 2017, www.buzzfeednews.com/article/bryanwashington/the-football-field-is-one-reality-america-is-another.

journal questions

1. Which of these stories impacted you most? Why?

2. How has/did the COVID-19 pandemic impact you? Your family? Your community?

3. What did you learn about yourself during the 2020/2021 pandemic?

4. Many have rightfully pointed out that COVID-19 amplified other societal problems in the United States (health care, policing, economic insecurities, immigrant rights, among others). How do these stories support that position? How do your personal observations and/or experiences reflect this position?

5. Many of the stories published in this volume end with a newfound perspective on one's abilities, capacities, and/or goals during the pandemic. Have you experienced any new insights or perspectives after experiencing the pandemic?

6. If you could interview one of the authors, who would you pick? Why? What would you ask that person?

7. Many have endured extreme challenges during the pandemic. Write about a time when you witnessed courage, love, and endurance during this crisis.

8. Write about a small or large victory that you experienced during the 2020/2021 pandemic.

9. Write about a small or large victory that your community achieved during the 2020/2021 pandemic.

10. Have you made any self-discoveries during the pandemic and/ or uprisings?

11. Moving forward, how would you address some of the issues described in these stories?

12. Reread the anthology's foreword "The Multiple Pandemics and Why We Fight" by Dr. Roberto D. Hernandez. Is there a specific line or passage that resonates with you? Can you draw any connections to your experiences or what you've witnessed during this challenging time in our history?

13. Did you participate in any of the 2020 protests? Describe what you heard, saw, and felt.

14. Darius Spearman's afterword "2020 Is the Culmination of a Generation of Disregard Toward the Poor and Most Vulnerable Among Us" concludes the anthology. How does his overview affect your thinking about what we've experienced during the pandemic and uprisings?

15. How do you feel about policing and/or prisons in the United States? Did any of the stories in the anthology change or support what you thought previously? Explain.